HOW TO READ

# Handwriting

# HOW TO READ
# Handwriting

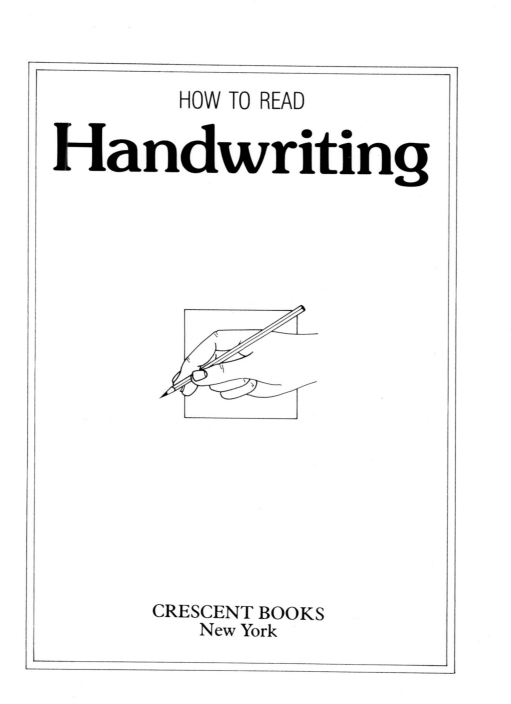

CRESCENT BOOKS
New York

This 1988 edition published by Crescent Books
Distributed by Crown Publishers Inc
225 Park Avenue South
New York
New York 10003

First published in the UK in 1988 by
Octopus Books Limited
Michelin House
81 Fulham Road
London SW3 6RB

Text and illustrations taken from the work
*Conoscerti, Enciclopedia dei Test*
© 1986 Gruppo Editoriale Fabbri SpA
Milan

© 1988 Octopus Books Limited

ISBN 0-517-66950-1

Printed and bound by Mandarin Offset in Hong Kong

hgfedcba

# Contents

Introduction 7

1 Basic Handwriting Features 11

2 Distinctive Letters 27

3 Personality Traits 37

4 Love 53

5 Summary 65

6 Dictionary of Graphology 79

Index 94

Acknowledgments 96

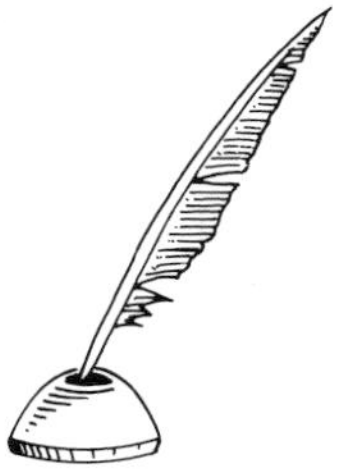

pudore : 7 operiantur sicut diploide
confusione sua

Confitebor domino nimis in
ore meo : et in medio multorum
laudabo eum

Qui astitit a dextris pauperis :
ut salvam faceret a persequentibz
animam meam

Gloria patri

Dñs Galfridus louterell me fieri
fecit

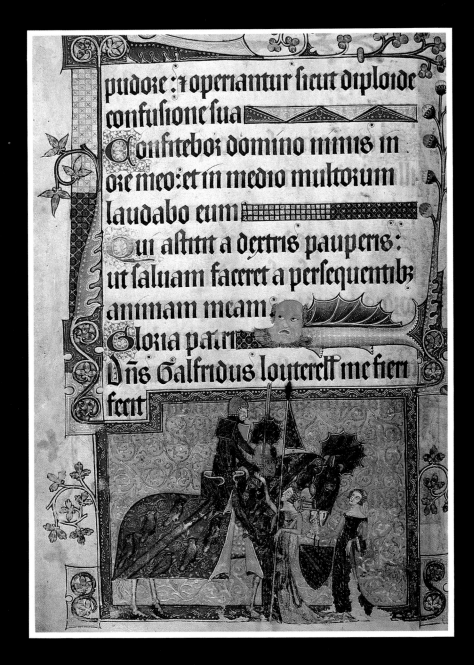

# Introduction

Graphology is sometimes regarded as an arcane science with little credibility, yet the first book on the subject was published as long ago as 1622 and it has remained in use up to the present time. Handwriting analysis is employed by the police worldwide and is accepted as evidence in criminal trials.

Long before the seventeenth century, references to characteristics of handwriting appeared in early literature. Its popularity waxed and waned according to the prevailing wisdom of the time, but although it became more obscure when reasoning and conclusive scientific proof were in the forefront of modern thought, it never died out.

Modern graphology as we know it was developed amongst the higher-ranking members of the French church in the mid-nineteenth century. Jean Hippolyte Michon, 'known as l'Abbé Michon, published three books on the subject between 1870 and 1875. He produced an extensive listing of signs but in those days, when psychology was yet to be discovered, his interpretations lacked any element of in-depth analysis of motivation and behaviour. His pupil, Jules Crépieux-Jamin, laid one of the foundation stones of modern graphology when he said that each sign can only be interpreted when considered in relation to the handwriting as a whole.

*A page from a book of psalms, commissioned by John Luttrell, the fourteenth century theologian*

With the development of psychology and psychoanalysis in Germany, more importance was attached to what graphology could reveal about the psyche of the writer. Just as a person betrays a wealth of information about his character by his gestures and posture, so he does by his handwriting. Someone with swift, sure movements will have correspondingly speedy and accurate handwriting; someone slow-moving and slow-thinking will also write slowly and carefully. The flourishing gestures of an exhibitionist will be mirrored in his handwriting, and even an amateur graphologist reading a letter from such a person will know what demeanour to expect from him on meeting.

This, of course, is the fascination of handwriting analysis. An insight into the character of a prospective employee (or employer) could play a decisive part in an appointment – indeed, employers frequently ask for handwritten letters of application. On a very basic level handwriting is easily interpreted as to the level of education and the capacity for neatness. On a more personal level, you could use it to gain a picture of a prospective lover's true nature. Most people, when looking for a partner, are on their best behaviour and a shock is sometimes in store when the real self comes to the fore – often when it is too late to turn back. Graphology can give you enough insight into another person's character to predict whether a future together might be possible.

You might also make some startling revelations about yourself. How we see ourselves is not always as others see us, and it sometimes seems that our capacity for self-delusion is limitless. You've probably listened to someone who is keen to tell you how unusual and eccentric he is, whereas you consider him conventional to a fault – or to someone tactless and aggressive announcing that he is the very model of diplomacy and peacefulness! Now is your chance to find out whether you, too, really are the person you believe yourself to be – and whether you see yourself as you would like to be, rather than as you really are.

You may well find that graphology helps to smooth your path through life You may discover that the reason you are not completely contented in your job is that your bent is for a completely different career. You may find that your friends have sensitivities you have not previously suspected and, with your new knowledge, you will be able to establish a more understanding relationship with them.

If you have children, you may be able to tell from their handwriting that they are having some difficulty, and, if so, you can treat the root of their problems early. As children grow and change, so will their handwriting: everyone's writing changes a little as their life evolves.

Graphology can never be an exact science; a change of mood on the part of the subject can alter his handwriting, so you should always ask for several samples written at different times. Most importantly, graphology stands or falls on the ability of the interpreter. To be a successful graphologist you need to have a basic understanding of human nature and the ability to leave no stone unturned as you assemble the different clues. When you are a beginner, it is all too easy to seize triumphantly upon telling features and ignore a host of other signs which modify or negate them. Needless to say, your own handwriting can even reveal how good a graphologist you will be! Broad letters (see page 18), systematic inequality (see page 38) and connection (see page 56) are all promising signs for your expertise in this field.

Once you have embarked on analysing handwriting, you will find that you are led deeper and deeper into this fascinating art as you discover the wealth of knowledge that is available to you. A knowledge of graphology makes it possible to delve into people's subconsciouses and, possibly, know more about them than they do themselves – maybe before you've even met them!

Mastering graphology to a professional standard requires extensive reading and study and unlimited experience; the British Institute of Graphology is outlining an official syllabus for graphology students to pave the way for academic recognition for graphology in this country. This book can by no means encompass all the aspects of graphology, but it will set you on the path of learning this ancient and valuable art.

1

# Basic Handwriting Features

Before you embark on a detailed examination of the form of a sample of handwriting, you should appreciate a few basic rules about graphology. If you are not fully aware of the way in which the signs can modify or negate each other you may well come to some very misleading conclusions! The conditions under which the sample is produced are important, too; giving someone a piece of lined paper and a biro and asking them to give you a sample for analysis will result in one that is unrepresentative and uninformative. This chapter lays down the guidelines which every graphologist must follow.

One of the easiest signs to recognize is whether the handwriting rises or falls as the writer's hand moves across the page, while the slant of the writing is probably one of the first things you notice. Up to now you have probably never paid these qualities any attention, but they are extremely revealing about the writer's character. Height and breadth of the letters is another sign which is easy to see – but you should remember that, although these signs may strike the eye immediately, graphology requires more exact measurements, since the intensity of the sign governs its meaning.

From this simple start you can move on to learning about stems and loops, fleeting gestures, and the significance of the capital letters.

Palazzo Pretorio *by Federico Zandomeneghi, the nineteenth century Italian painter*

# Ten golden rules

The analysis of handwriting is governed by 10 funda-mental rules that you must bear in mind at all times; it's not enough just to know the meaning of the various graph-ological signs in order to assess a script correctly. The rules are the foundation of an accurate analysis.

No doubt the first handwriting you will want to analyse will be your own, but it is helpful to take a look at the signatures of some famous figures whose personalities are well-established. Examples of them throughout this book will help you recognize certain handwriting features.

1  Every graphological sign has its own specific mean-ing and never represents different or opposite trends.

2  Every graphological sign is indicative of facets of the intelligence, character and physique.

3  Each graphological sign may be reinforced, dimin-ished or neutralized when combined with other signs that are confirmatory, contrary or neutral respectively; it can thus acquire different meanings and become complex, even though it is simple in itself.

4  The meaning of each graphological sign is the same for both men and women, although in women it is likely to relate more to the emotions than to the intelligence and vice versa in men. This is not, of course, a categorical statement, and you should not use it to jump to conclusions or you may be led astray. It is something to bear in mind if many other features also suggest this.

5  The percentage of each graphological sign, cal-culated in tenths, must be measured so that you can define mathematically whether this is below or above average. When a feature is present to its full extent, it is calculated as 10/10, or 100 per cent. If it is shown to a lesser extent, it may be calculated as anything between 1/10 and 9/10; simple guidelines and examples throughout this book will help you decide to what extent a piece of handwriting reveals any particular trait. However, keep a flexible attitude to this as minor variations are attributable to slight changes in mood.

6  The personality and character of the writer can be established from the sum of all of the graphological signs examined and evaluated in conjunction with the modifying signs. Never make an evaluation on the basis of only one or two features present. This would give an inaccurate, and, possibly, damaging view of a subject's personality.

7  Every graphological sign expresses a constant value and may be defined as essential, modifying or inci-dental. Essential signs reflect the writer's character make-up; modifying signs make the essential signs more or less incisive; and incidental signs back up the meaning of the first two signs. Remember that the conditional force of each sign influences the others and that their combination determines the balance of characteristics revealed in the handwriting.

8  Graphology reveals mental characteristics, intellec-tual properties and behavioural tendencies.

9  A high percentage of a given graphological sign renders the script particularly significant; if it relates to the willpower it predominates over and affects all other signs in relation to both the willpower and to the intellect. If an essential sign and a modifying sign are equally apparent the former will predominate, giving its own particular indication of the personality.

If a modifying sign is present to a greater extent than the essential sign that it should be modifying, it takes precedence and imposes its own characteristics. Similarly if an incidental sign is present in a greater percentage than the essential and modifying signs it indicates personality traits of its own: if the sign that predominates in the sphere of the willpower is an essential sign the personality will be decisive and solid, fired by deep-rooted vital energy; if the predominant sign is a modifying sign the personality will be less structured but more complicated, the characterizing force not being direct but reflected; if the predominant sign is an incidental sign the personality will be delicate, and lacking in forcefulness.

10  Finally, it must be remembered that the only type of script that can be regarded as valid for the purposes of serious interpretation is a script produced sponta-neously and naturally, with no external pressure of any kind and no deliberate camouflaging by its author.

## Jean Paul Marat

The signature of Marat, the famous 'friend of the people' killed by Charlotte Corday during the French revolution, denotes courage and clarity of ideas. The upstroke indicates enterprise, the bottom loop the desire to make other people embrace his own cause.

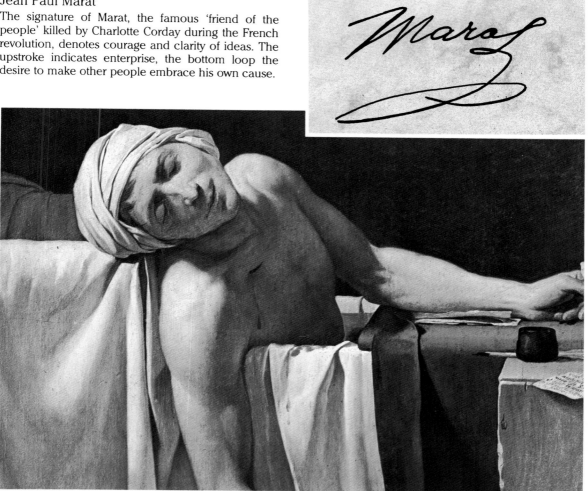

The Dead Marat, *1793, by Jacques-Louis David, the eighteenth century French painter*

## Jacqueline Kennedy

Jacqueline Kennedy's signature shows a certain tendency towards introversion. A notable characteristic is the leftward lean of the letters. This tendency is reinforced by the leftward extension of the end stroke of the 'q', an indication of the writer's reluctance to open up to others and of a desire to protect the inner self. The large capital letters and emphasized upstroke reveal a decisive, independent personality with an ability to put herself forward.

# The signature

The graphological signs of a person's signature are often influenced by a quest for beauty and originality, so care needs to be taken when evaluating it. Everyone has applied themselves to fashioning their own signature at some time in their youth. It is their own personal stamp and as such they may want it to be unusual and decorative; it therefore often contains an element of exhibitionism. Visually the signature represents a person's idea of what he or she is like – not what he or she is actually like.

It has been pointed out that the signatures of the great men of history, and particularly those of politicians and military leaders, are only spontaneous at times of difficulty. Only then does the handwriting drop the mask that has been used to keep the world at bay and appear as it really is, with its merits and weaknesses.

The comment is an interesting one, and it does contain a certain amount of truth; Napoleon's signature on the day after the battle of Waterloo is little more than hieroglyphics, pointing gloomily downwards, and quite different from the proud scrawl pointing towards the sky on the notice of victory at Austerlitz. Hitler's signature on his defeat, written in the bunker in Berlin, surges to the right in a maniacal fashion, while when he had just invaded Poland it was hysterical and impetuous.

However, the signature, like handwriting, contains certain personal features which neither the passage of time nor a change in fortunes can annul. The signatures shown here are in isolation, but much can also be revealed by examining the signature in relation to the text. This will show whether what the individual thinks he or she is like is in accordance with the persons he or she presents to society. A skilled and intuitive graphologist can at any time draw a truthful picture of the personality of the signator. Judges in more than one famous trial have made use of expert assessments of the accused's signature as well as his or her handwriting. Graphology is rapidly acquiring the dignity of a science all over the world and in Argentina there is already a university chair in the subject.

Remember that the ability to read graphological signs correctly requires practice and application and has to be acquired in stages, not learned in a rush of enthusiasm. When, for example, the handwriting being examined is of the rising type (typical of enterprise), this does not necessarily mean that the characteristic tendencies of this feature apply because, if the rising handwriting is accompanied by exaggerated stems, the writer may have a tendency towards obstinacy, intransigence, and an inflated sense of his own importance – it all depends on how pronounced the signs are, and to what extent they are offset by others.

## Winston Churchill
This is the signature of someone who is accustomed to taking decisions independently of others, whom he keeps at a distance. The handwriting is fast and assured and perfectly straight, indicating a well-balanced individual.

## Leonardo da Vinci
The form of the letters leaves no room for doubt: this is an individual who is particularly predisposed towards applied arts and mathematics.

## Adolph Hitler
His signature is that of an individual afflicted by phobias and complexes of a sexual nature. Hitler's unquestionable intellectual acuity was obscured by a disproportionate arrogance and a tendency to daydream.

## John F. Kennedy
An energetic signature like this one shows a person accustomed to considering others to be at his service. John F. Kennedy loved popularity, was unscrupulous in politics, and considered himself irresistible to women.

*Portrait of Napoleon Bonaparte, Emperor of France*

### Napoleon

This is the signature of a man of action – shown by the rightward direction – but also of a thinking man. It suggests possible problems in the sexual sphere. At the start of his military career, Napoleon used to sign documents extremely carefully, saying that he wanted to give a positive impression of himself in his signature.

People in the public eye often create a special signature – their fame goes hand in hand with a desire to express their egos. A large signature shows self importance, whereas one which is the same size as the rest of a person's handwriting, and written in the same style, reveals that this person's idea of himself or herself matches what he or she is really like. A signature may diminish in size or slope downwards after a disappointment – as did Napoleon's after the battle of Waterloo. The added embellishment of an underline denotes a certain amount of showmanship.

---

### Remember these rules

Before embarking on the analysis of the essential elements of handwriting, which are referred to as graphological signs, it is useful to establish a few basic precepts.

In order to gain a true picture of the subject's personality it is worth first of all ensuring that the conditions under which the handwriting was produced were right.

1 Make sure that the writer used a pen containing liquid ink (this will show up the pressure exerted on the paper and the thickness of the letters drawn).
2 It is essential to use white, unlined paper with no margins (this will show the direction of the handwriting).
3 It is preferable to evaluate a specimen that has been produced spontaneously rather than specifically for graphological analysis.
4 The content of the written text is always totally irrelevant.

# The slant

There are characteristic graphological features of three basic types of handwriting: rising handwriting, straight handwriting and falling handwriting.

### Rising handwriting
This type of handwriting, which moves away from the line in an upward direction, denotes a tendency towards excess energy which is not controlled by willpower. To establish the characteristic indicated you need to consider the other tendencies with which excess energy is associated: if it is combined with a generous, open temperament, it becomes optimism; where combined with superficial intelligence and vanity it becomes arrogance; and where combined with excellent intellectual abilities and a strong will it becomes a tendency to improve oneself.

### Straight handwriting
This indicates an iron will and resoluteness. The maximum level of this type of handwriting (measured in tenths) is found when, if a line is drawn underneath it, the script is seen to keep perfectly to the line. This feature, depending on its intensity, denotes the level of ability to control the temperament by strength of will. It may be said to be typical of balanced, self-controlled people.

### Falling handwriting
Handwriting that falls below the line is an indication of a weak will and lack of moral fibre. It is thus a characteristic feature of people who are mentally fragile with a tendency towards depression, unease and loss of confidence in themselves and in others. Here again the extent to which the handwriting falls needs to be considered. When it is 2/10 falling the subject may simply be prone to melancholy, but when it is 8/10 falling he or she has severe emotional difficulties. In all cases the sign has to be interpreted within a broader context.

### Forced handwriting
Handwriting tending to the left in all cases indicates a difficulty on the part of the writer in communicating and projecting himself on the outside world. A slant towards the right, on the contrary, means a readiness to relate to everything and everyone.

When a script shows uniform distortion the graphological sign is that of forced handwriting. This distortion does not derive from a choice on the part of the writer, but from an aversion to and uneasiness in his environment and among the people that he lives with. The sensation of unease is revealed by handwriting leaning to the left or by elongated stems, bending backwards.

Taken as a whole, the sign reveals narrow mental channelling. These people suffer from rigid constraint in their learning processes and are unable to concentrate their attention on more than one element at a time. They have difficulty in comprehension and in absorbing new ideas. They tend to distort reality and to make highly subjective judgements.

Individuals with this sign are indecisive and lack common sense, practicality and an ability to overcome obstacles. Their imagination is limited and they lack creativity.

Emotionally, they are tense and suppressed and thus suffer frequent bouts of nervous exhaustion. Although they are limited in their emotions they have at the same time an extreme need for affection, its absence causing them a sense of inferiority and bouts of irritability. They have trouble in choosing how to spend their free time, having no particular interests.

*Forced handwriting sloping leftwards suggests the writer has difficulty communicating*

### Distorted handwriting
Like forced handwriting, distorted handwriting is regular, but in this case it is regular in the pronounced distortion of certain letters when compared with the copybook style. These letters, however, still remain legible.

Unlike forced handwriting, which suggests the writer is discontented, distortion reveals freedom of choice on the part of the writer in forming his or her letters in a very unusual way. Those with this sign experience difficulty in concentrating and in comprehension and tend to be indecisive. In terms of their emotions they are tense and easily irritated, with moments of sadness and unease that give them a pessimistic view of any situation. They have unusual tastes and often appear to be in conflict with the choices made by those around them, making life awkward for themselves and for others.

*Portrait of the publisher, Stephen Jones, 1782 from Sir and Lady Inglefield's Collection, Bedfordshire*

# Height and breadth

Another way of establishing the character traits of the writer is by studying the relationship between the height and breadth of the letters, particularly the rounded ones such as 'a' and 'o'. These letters, when the graphological sign applies to the maximum extent, are as broad as they are high.

*Letters which are as broad as they are high indicate intelligence*

The degree of intensity of the sign is expressed as a fraction in which the denominator is the number of millimetres in height and the numerator the number of millimetres in breadth. The fraction is then converted into tenths. This procedure will present no particular difficulty once you have had some practice.

Downstrokes in handwriting relate to willpower, upstrokes are linked to feelings and horizontal strokes are associated with intelligence.

## Broad letters

The extension of the horizontal line, seen when the letter is more rounded than necessary, indicates a capability for intellectual action that is balanced by strength of will and emotions. In this case, the writer has a good grasp of reality without being unduly swayed by his feelings. A person with the graphological sign of broad letters has profound intelligence, is able to develop complex ideas of his or her own, finds it easy to concentrate, has good powers of expression and has an aptitude for scientific and theoretical research.

Such people respect their own inner feelings and those of others and take relationships seriously, detesting superficiality of any kind. Seven and eight tenths of the sign are excellent; a greater percentage will alter the values, as excessive elongation of the horizontal stroke means a loss of balance between the horizontal stroke and the upstrokes and downstrokes, meaning that this person is somewhat self-indulgent, egotistic, tends to act on a whim and can be inconsiderate.

## Narrow letters

When the letters are less than five-tenths in breadth, the handwriting may be regarded as having the feature of narrow letters. Such writing is sometimes described as concentrated. This feature is generally combined with those of sharp and spiky handwriting.

Sharp handwriting shows little horizontal extension, with acute angles at the tops of letters such as 'A' and 'B'. A person with this sign shows sharp intelligence but lacks theoretical depth. He or she will grasp concepts quickly but lacks vision and may lose sight of the central core of the problem.

These subjects can generally find people's weaknesses and can be ironic and sarcastic. On the other hand they suffer when they believe that other people do not respect them. Being in the habit of upholding their own point of view at all costs, they could make excellent barristers or be successful in jobs in which they have to convince others to share their opinions.

The characteristics of sharp writing are accentuated in spiky handwriting. The upper and lower angles of the rounded letters are extremely pointed, to such an extent that the upstroke almost coincides with the downstroke. This feature is indicative of a poor grasp of reality, a readiness to accept things at surface value, and a tendency to propound one's own ideas. These writers are always at odds with themselves and with others, by whom they feel themselves to be rejected. When only certain words in a text are narrow, this shows a source of grievance – which is usually indicated by the very words which are narrow.

*Writing which has the feature of narrow letters is often spiky*

## Alfred Nobel

Alfred Nobel, the Swedish chemist and industrialist, was born in Stockholm in 1833. He studied in St Petersburg, where his father was director of the dockyards, and returned to his home country in 1859. He was particularly interested in the use of nitroglycerine as an explosive, and in 1863 he began to manufacture it in a small laboratory near Stockholm. He also worked in Paris, where he carried out research into improving dynamite, and, finally, in 1890, in San Remo. His name, however, remains linked primarily to the Nobel Prize, which he instigated by decreeing in his will that virtually the whole of his estate should be used to set up a foundation of five prizes per year to be awarded to those 'who have rendered the greatest service to mankind'. The foundation came into being in 1896. Nobel's signature shows pomposity, evinced by the elaborate capitals and underlining. Yet the width and clarity of his style also reveal intelligence.

*Guglielmo Marconi, Italian inventor and physicist*

## Guglielmo Marconi

Guglielmo Marconi, a great Italian scientist, was born in Bologna in 1874 of an Italian father and an Irish mother. He completed his initial studies in Bologna and Florence, working in physics and electronics. When Marconi began his experiments in 1894, all of the fundamental properties of electromagnetic waves were already known. Two years later he moved to Britain in a quest for funds and his system of telegraphic transmission was patented in London. A decisive step was taken when Marconi mounted a practical demonstration of how to overcome the curvature of the earth in radio-telegraph transmissions. He won the Nobel Prize for physics in 1909. His autograph indicates simplicity, tenacity and intuition, while the broad letters denote his ability to think clearly.

# Curls

Curls, like dots, accents and underlining, are the expressions of 'fleeting gestures' – clues to the character and personality. The fleeting gesture is shown primarily in the most characteristic and spontaneous attitudes of each individual, and may be particularly revealing in the case of someone who is trying to conceal his true nature.

In handwriting, the fleeting gesture chiefly takes the form of curls, found mainly at the start of words but also occasionally occurring in the middle or at the end. However the term also includes 't' crosses, dots and accents, underlining and flourishes.

The fleeting gesture bears a distinct relation to the overall character of the writing: the curl of sobriety will only be found in plain handwriting, the curl of confusion only in contorted handwriting and the curl of arrogance only in pretentious handwriting.

Understanding the fleeting gesture will help to identify the intrinsic nature of the personality. Each individual may use a variety of gestures, although they are always in line with the characteristics relating to the overall combination of signs.

The term curl is used to signify the starting or ending strokes of letters, and those forming an integral part of the letter as in the case of the 't' cross, dots or accents, often made outside the letter or word.

## The curl of concealment

This is found when the final stroke of the word bends hook-like under the last letter, turning back towards the left. The length of the hook is unimportant: it is generally relatively short. The frequency of the curl gives the percentage intensity of the sign. If all last letters of words have a curl, the sign applies 10/10; a 90 per cent frequency gives 9/10, and so on.

*The curl of concealment – the last stroke hooks back and under*

The curl of concealment denotes a tendency on the part of the writer to conceal the real self behind a screen of reserve and reticence. He or she does not formulate any judgements and never makes any categorical statements in order to avoid possible arguments. Even if, in the final analysis, the writer is not a liar, he or she is nonetheless reticent in telling the truth. If involved in any underhand or slightly dishonest activities this person will avoid owning up, leaving others to carry the can.

Those with this sign will look at people extremely attentively so that nothing escapes their enquiring and wary eyes; they will not allow themselves to be taken unawares and are always cautious. They are circumspect and diffident in their appearance, too; their voices are modulated, their carriage determined, but they are on guard. Their gestures are controlled and their approach to others is courteous but devoid of warmth or expression.

*Handwriting with the curl of concealment reflects a secretive self*

Subjects with a curl of concealment are unlikely to reveal their passions: even if they feel violent anger or a desire for revenge they will not explode openly and will act without making themselves noticeable. In disputes they will give no view of any kind and it is never possible to determine their true opinion. They are aloof and do not attract confidences from others.

Those with this sign are suited to carrying out tasks requiring secrecy. They can establish other people's positions without revealing their own, and are able to maintain relationships of formal courtesy and diplomacy with anyone.

If the curl of concealment is found in precise handwriting, typical of a lack of spontaneity, it accentuates the tendency towards insincerity and falsehood and indicates a desire to conceal the writer's true self from others which will undoubtedly derive from the formative years.

A child who has curls of concealment in his or her handwriting should be encouraged to express ideas and thoughts sincerely and openly. He or she should be given enough reassurance to feel able to take up his or her own stand and assume responsibilities in order to lose the fear of what he or she regards as inadmissible weaknesses being discovered.

# Stems and loops

The distinction between the way in which stems and loops are written is essential in determining the writer's ability to distinguish between right and wrong.

Stems and loops are essentially strokes drawn above and below the level of the rounded letters; generally they follow a different line. The degree of difference between them indicates the writer's ability to distinguish between the morally acceptable and unacceptable.

If the same path is followed in writing both stems and loops, this means that the writer is unable to grasp the particular features distinguishing two similar situations. The maximum degree of discernment is shown when the stems form a sharp angle of approximately 85–90° with the loops.

### Wide-apart stems and loops

Writers with wide-apart stems and loops will have a good memory, will be able to discard irrelevant ideas and are not prone to making mistakes. They will have extreme clarity of thought. In romantic relationships they will steer clear of any attachments that are socially frowned upon and they dislike promiscuity. They feel the need to have a clear conscience at all times, and like to move in an environment that is free from dishonesty and intrigue.

These people attach a lot of importance to their appearance and to cleanliness and hygiene. They shop cautiously with an eye to economy and are unlikely to waste anything.

*A tidy person with good recall may have wide-apart writing*

### Close stems and loops

When there is no difference between the course of the stems and the loops, the handwriting is described as muddled.

The predominant characteristics expressed by this sign are intellectual and emotional confusion. A person with this sign lacks concentration and is easily confused by situations where the correct course of action is not immediately obvious. This is because the downward and upward strokes of the stems and loops respectively correspond to mental and physical activity, which are linked but should not be confused. Such people rarely learn from past experiences and they can be particularly unpredictable.

*Muddled handwriting denotes confused ideas and feelings*

The haphazard way in which such people live causes them to make mistakes and to suffer from misunderstandings that often prejudice their working relationships and their love lives, which are marked by lack of communication and frequent quarrels. Their actions are not always consistent with what they themselves have said, as they do not clearly remember what that was.

Those with this sign are very talkative, often to excess, and when it comes to making decisions they cannot concentrate their attention on what is relevant. Because of their lack of organization their efforts are often doomed to failure and they use up energy to no avail. They lack self-criticism and find it difficult to change their minds or question their actions. They tend to be too proud and arrogant.

In their affections, too, they suffer from uncertainty. They show a tendency towards anger and irrationality and do not always take due care of themselves, either in the way they dress or in their personal hygiene. These are people of fragile psychology, who easily become victims of their own mental confusion.

A child with a high degree of intensity of this sign is in urgent need of guidance in order to be able to overcome the uncertainties and hesitations characteristic of his or her behaviour. He or she should be surrounded by the calm and serenity necessary to push his or her confusion, and everything that it entails, into the background, or at least to control it.

# Capital letters

Capital letters, in addition to being used at the beginning of a sentence, are also used for the first letters of surnames and forenames, bearing witness to the importance attributed to them in relation to the rest of the words in the sentence.

## Large capitals
When the capital letters are large and ornate and some of the other letters look as if they themselves are capitals, this may be described as conceited movement; it goes without saying that the most obvious characteristic of these writers is a generally conceited attitude. If others fail to give them the respect they feel they deserve they will be liable to outbursts of anger. In writing a flourishing signature they think they are presenting themselves to others as people of importance, and the space that they are given to write in never seems to them to be sufficient.

A distinctive feature of people with this sign is extreme independence and an exaggerated view of their own abilities. They will tend to regard themselves as their own master in taking decisions and making choices, based on the conviction that it would be impossible for them to make a mistake. They find it difficult to admit their mistakes and are never self-critical.

In terms of their personal relationships, they are unable to accept criticism from those around them. If they are crossed, they are likely to fly into a rage and even to react violently. When it comes to sex, they are more concerned with their own pleasure than with that of their partner.

*Large capitals, as might be expected, indicate a conceited nature*

In bringing up their children they tend to be domineering and have no scruples in denigrating others in order to boost their own image. They are arrogant and lack the necessary balance to be able to make objective judgements.

Briefly, people who have this sign will always be carried away by their unbridled egocentricity and will never succeed in performing a single act of modesty or humility.

If they occupy roles of command they abuse their power and give free reign to their arrogance, becoming high-handed, overbearing and sometimes even violent. They thus cause themselves to be disliked by those around them, and their stressful relationships often make them isolated and neurotic.

## Backward slanting capitals
Capital letters which, in addition to being large, also show a leftward movement, indicate a retrospective outlook on the part of the writer. In graphology, this is given the name of 'backward movement'. Its intensity is calculated on how frequently it occurs throughout a person's handwriting.

*Chaplin was buried in a little cemetery overlooking lake Geneva in Switzerland*

*Backward slanting capitals signal a preoccupation with the past*

The main characteristic expressed by this sign is a morbid attachment to past experiences. People who write like this fantasize on the past and on events long gone by, living them with the same intensity as that with which others throw themselves into the present. They have a vivid memory, even for the tiniest details of past events, which they can recall at any moment.

Just as they can collect and tabulate memories, so they are able to collect and catalogue objects of different kinds. They also show excellent ability in keeping records, and are well suited to any job which involves collating data such as librarianship or clerical work.

In terms of their love lives, these writers live by their memories of relationships which, as time goes by, assume even greater importance. They are thus quite likely to live lives of regrets and nostalgia. It is very difficult for them to forget their disappointments and they are also quite inflexible when it comes to moving away from places where they have particularly enjoyed living or comes to leaving a job to start another one.

# The graphologist

*For hundreds of years, glasses have been made in many shapes and sizes.*

*Handwriting characterized by broad letters with average spacing between them is the sign of an investigative mind – and a good graphologist*

Anyone who wishes to investigate other people's personalities through their handwriting must have a well-balanced character. Another essential trait of the graphologist is reserve – otherwise it would be dangerous to work on other people.

Once a basic knowledge of the graphological signs and their meaning has been acquired, the skilled graphologist needs a set of useful rules for analysing handwriting correctly. Handwriting is a projection of personality. In order to discover a personality, the graphologist must analyse the course of the graphic act, identify the most significant signs, understand the meaning and value of handwriting and explore its inner rhythm as if trying to penetrate the innermost psychology of the writer. The greater the depth of this investigation, the more appropriate the perception of the personality being explored.

Whilst the individual's personality can be extrapolated from a spontaneous script, his or her development can also be deduced from a series of scripts produced in different circumstances and at different times. The graphologist needs to have theoretical powers and an in-depth knowledge of graphology in its widest sense: the individual's personality will be reconstructed on the basis of the information provided by the graphological signs present in his or her handwriting. Certain signs should characterize the handwriting of the graphologist:

## Breadth of letters
If the breadth of the letters is above average it shows intellectual depth: the writer will be able to penetrate other people's minds intelligently.

## Spacing between letters
If this is about average it will provide an indication of powers of fair judgement and the ability to remain impartial and detached in evaluating the facts.

## Spacing between words
Above average word spacing, but at a lesser percentage than the breadth of letters, will denote critical powers which are essential to the individual's personality.

These first three signs are extremely important, and must coexist in harmony. In addition a size that is somewhat small, or at least not greater than average, will denote a spirit of observation in the graphologist, and an ability to notice things that escape less attentive eyes. A marked fluidity of style gives him or her quick and immediate powers of intuition and psychological talent: these are essential characteristics for understanding other people through the signs and messages that they send to the outside world.

The sign of cleverness is systematic inequality (see page 38). If above average, it will provide a wealth of enlightenment enabling the most disparate characteristics, possibly worthy of little attention, to be understood with flair and imagination. Types of handwriting without excessive breaks denote powers of synthesis and analysis and an ability to consider circumstances in detail and to give an overall view of them. Similarly the graphologist should not be easily influenced and should be moderately independent. These characteristics are revealed in uprightness or a slight right hand slant, with straight stems.

The sign of clarity will show a graphologist who has the ability to keep assessments as clear as possible and formulate accurate judgements and opinions – especially necessary when handwriting provides the writer with an indication of activities to pursue or directions to follow in the future.

Noticeable plainness and spontaneous precision will also provide the analyst with sobriety and incisiveness of language. In formulating your assessments you must not be misunderstood. The one constant feature in the handwriting of a person wishing to assess other people's handwriting is moderation. The graphological signs, even those that express positive traits, are never found at their maximum levels. Signs that in any way express morbid or pathological situations must not be present: these would result in a loss of lucidity and objectiveness in psychological investigation. When ascertaining the most intimate aspects of the writer's character, it would be dangerous to work on others without being able to assure them of a minimum level of professionalism and reserve.

# Analysing handwriting

*The graphologist should be supplied with as much writing, on unlined paper, as possible: several sheets of a letter would be ideal.*

*Writing that is done especially for analysis is not suitable: an inevitable amount of self - consciousness would affect important formations such as t bars, i dots and loops.*

Graphology is primarily a practical skill. To test your newly-acquired knowledge a step-by-step handwriting analysis, incorporating some of the basic elements of graphology discussed in this chapter, will show you how theory works in practice.

At first glance this handwriting sample appears deceptively simple; it is clear, even and unadorned. Looking more closely, a much more complicated character begins to emerge. The writer is a 25 year old woman, working in advertising.

First examine the primary direction of the handwriting in relation to the line. To do this, look at the base line – it will help you to draw a straight line with a ruler beneath the sentences. Does the handwriting ascend, descend, or curve in any way? The sample provides examples of all three tendencies – resulting in a slightly wavy base line – indicative of a flexible outlook. Here is someone who is responsive to the world about her, energetic, and open to new ideas.

Now consider the direction of the slope, if any. Again, where this is not immediately apparent a ruler helps. Simply draw some vertical lines through the sample at various points, and the subtlest slope will be revealed – as it is here. Although this handwriting appears vertical, a very slight forward lean is also evident.

Predominantly vertical handwriting signals an independent, thoughtful person whose careful judgement and self-control are invaluable in any emergency. Additionally, minimal forward leaning tendencies reveal a self-reliant personality who would welcome responsibility. She would work most productively as the head of a team, or on her own: inclines in handwriting signal basic character inclinations. Handwriting which leans forward, therefore, shows an inclination to action – just as a backward sloping style suggests someone who is bound to the past.

Size and spacing are vital elements in graphology. Size reliably indicates basic personality type, while the spacing between words and letters shows how the individual behaves in relation to others. This medium-sized specimen endorses the conclusions drawn so far by showing a balanced approach – neither markedly extrovert, nor painfully shy.

The spacing between individual words in the sample is quite wide, averaging 4 millimetres. This sign reinforces those indications of self-sufficiency and an ability to think rationally before taking action which were initially revealed by the direction of the handwriting. While the spacing between each letter is fairly wide, demonstrating

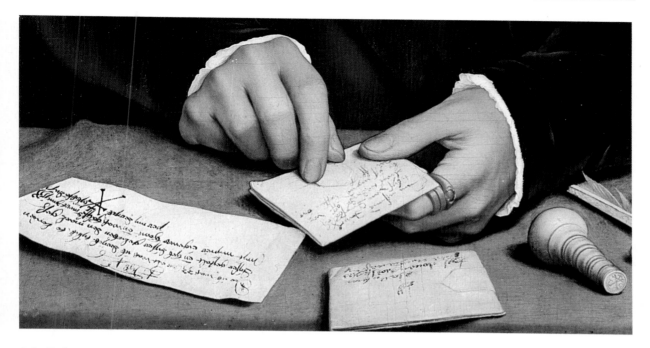

*A detail of a painting from the Flemish school, showing the graphologist at work*

an outgoing attitude towards others, widely-spaced words reveal that this person also needs privacy from time to time.

Having analysed the size, spacing, and direction of the handwriting, you should look at its overall shape. Is it rounded, or does it have an angular appearance? Much adult handwriting contains elements of both signs, for as children develop into adults their handwriting becomes more individual, expressing the complexity of a mature personality.

This woman has clearly been taught a basic, unpretentious style, to which she has added both angular and curved letters. Rounded writing denotes an emotional, flexible person who is sympathetic and understanding. The additional angular element means that while she is undoubtedly kind, she is also clever and observant. Her ability to be objective is underlined by the clarity and width of the individual letters, whose simplicity further indicates someone both practical and intelligent.

Stems and loops are analysed both for their shape, and as upper and lower extensions in the handwriting. A combination of looped letters and simple strokes, as illustrated by this handwriting, reveals a slightly repressed imagination. Creativity is expressed in primarily down-to-earth ways. Looking at the lower extensions, particularly the letters 'g' and 'y', you can see indications of a strongly instinctual nature. Since the upper extensions are not

especially emphasized, the essential practicality of this individual is confirmed. Here is someone who would enjoy physical comforts and activities, but whose instincts might fight an inner battle with her more logical thought processes.

The capital letters in our specimen help to explain why the subject doesn't fully express herself, for they denote a lack of self-confidence: these letters are quite small when compared to the rest of the writing – indicating a conscientious, slightly reserved person. Their simple form also reinforces other signs of objectivity – and suggests efficiency too.

Having completed your first analysis, a broad character sketch has been created from a sample of handwriting. This initial psychological exploration can be deepened by examining individual letters and signs, such as 't' bars, which are explained in the following chapter. It would be interesting on your first assessment also to examine the signature of the subject, as the signature gives you an idea of how someone sees themselves. You may also find that other handwriting features discussed in this chapter, which are not noteworthy in this example, are of importance in the piece of handwriting which you analyse. The example revealed a very positive, well-balanced personality with few problems: later chapters show you how to evaluate the many complex contradictory tendencies reflected by handwriting.

# 2

# Distinctive Letters

There are certain letters in graphology which hold particular significance. Those with stems, such as b, f, h, l, p and t, carry a wealth of information about the writer; the stems may be upright, forward curving or backward curving, and each style holds its own meaning. Generally the stems compensate for, accentuate or negate tendencies expressed by other handwriting features. The 't' holds further interest in the way the cross is formed – for example, an extended cross pointed towards the top reveals a liar, while a low, short, heavy cross is the sign of serenity and generosity. A thin 't' cross betrays a weak-willed individual who is always eager to stay on the right side of other people.

Other important signs of a person's character are seen in the upstrokes and downstrokes of such letters. The length, calculated in relation to the size of the oval of a letter, determines the meaning. A perfect balance between the two is the ideal, meaning that the self, the intellect and the instincts are in perfect equilibrium.

In graphology even minute details are accounted for, and the dot over the 'i' can tell you a lot. It may be low, high, to the right, a dash rather than a dot – take a look at your own to see which category it falls into. Always remember, though, that a sign should never be considered in isolation, but in relation to the others.

*Detail of a page from a seventh century Irish book of psalms*

# Stemmed letters

In order to analyse handwriting correctly you need to evaluate all graphological features together. If the handwriting you are analysing has a downward slope, for example, this shows a tendency towards a weak will and a lack of determination. If, on the other hand, the same handwriting exhibits a particular kind of irregularity you may be able to say that the individual in question makes up for his lack of will by a commitment to his ideas and a sharp intelligence.

The contribution of the graphological feature of the upright, forward curving and backward curving stem is generally to compensate for, accentuate or cancel out the tendencies expressed by other features. For this type of analysis the stems of the letters t, l, b, f, h and p are mainly used.

To establish whether a stem is upright, forward curving or backward curving, take a 't' and draw a vertical line from the base to the tip of the letter and you will see immediately whether or not the line coincides with the stems of the letter. If the line coincides with the stem, the stem is upright: if the stem slants towards the reader's right it is forward curving, and if it slants towards the reader's left it is backward curving.

If a given specimen of handwriting exhibits only one type of stem, then the feature applies to a level of 10/10: if, on the other hand, there are two or more different types of stem, you will need to take an average in order to determine the percentage of each.

## Upright stems
Upright strokes indicate a tendency towards inflexibility (not the same as resoluteness, which is denoted by writing that keeps to a horizontal course). They also indicate independence of thought and feelings.

Individuals with a high proportion of this type of feature are rigid and uncompromising; they are inflexible, and remain so even when subjected to outside pressure. They see their own particular methods and ideas as the only valid ones. They show the same rigidity in their evaluation of events: they are not prepared to consider attenuating circumstances, and restrict themselves to analysing reality as it appears without dwelling on the determining causes. It is hardly surprising if these individuals prove to be despots both in relation to others and to themselves. With their intransigence, they are certainly not easy people to get along with, but they do have one great virtue: they are incorruptible.

An excessive proportion of this feature is negative, while a value of around 7/10, or a combination with curves and broadness in other letters, indicating kindness,

means that these individuals are honest and faithful to their ideals and affections.

*Notice the upright stems of the letters – an indication of rigidity*

## Forward curving stems
Forward curving strokes with the concave part to the right ('t') indicate compliancy in both judgement and behaviour. Compliancy here is taken in the sense of an ability to show flexibility of judgement by taking all factors of a situation into account. An individual whose handwriting shows this feature welcomes other people's confidences, and the greater the proportion of perpendicular stems also to be found in the handwriting, the greater the person's discretion.

## Backward curving stems
Backward curving stems with the concave part to the reader's left ('d') have the opposite meaning to forward curving stems. This is a feature that indicates a rejection of other people's feelings and ideas and a tendency towards diffidence. Any people with this feature in a large proportion will find it difficult to accept others' suggestions. It is almost as if they feel that they are being forced to accept something alien to their own way of life and so withdraw, feeling that they have to take up a defensive position. Individuals of this type will only appear to accept innovation; in reality, they are born conservatives.

When the left curving stem feature is combined with sharp handwriting and narrow spacing between letters, the tendencies expressed are heightened. On the other hand, when a proportion of curves and right curving stems are present, the tendencies expressed by left curving stems are moderated by these two features, which indicate softness and pliability.

As you learn more about handwriting analysis you will find it easy to identify the combinations of contradictory features that modify each other.

# Crossing the 't'

*Quite simply, pasta means dough, a plain substance made from flour, water and salt. The flour is that milled from*

*Handwriting with long 't' crosses belongs to a powerful and passionate person with few inhibitions*

According to Crépieux-Jamin (see page 7), there are 40 different forms of 't' cross. It is believed that they provide the graphologist with information of considerable importance in assessing the signs contained in a script. In addition, these crosses can be easily identified, being instantly recognizable and assessable with no possibility of confusion or uncertainty.

### The form of the cross

One thing that is certain is that the 't' cross is in line with the graphic dynamism of the entire script being examined: you will find that a script that is plain and small will have short stroke 't' crosses carefully positioned in copybook fashion, while in lavish or tall handwriting the 't' crosses will tend to be long and written with a certain amount of haste. A script that contains the indicative curls of a liar will have extended crosses that are pointed towards the top, while a bold script will have decisive crosses, developed towards the right-hand part of the stem of the 't'.

In a script that is both joined and thread-like the crosses will be found to exhibit a triangular bend at the end of the stroke, starting the next letter, as if the writer is so absorbed by the rhythm and continuity of his or her thoughts and he or she cannot afford to make any breaks or interruptions. If the script is joined and flowing, and also shows graphological signs of impatience (see page 48), the 't' crosses may be omitted in the writer's haste.

Handwriting which shows signs of calm and tranquillity (see page 48) generally has 't's' in which the crosses are discreet, possibly starting from the line and intersecting the stem in the shape of a letter 'x'. Contrastingly short, heavy crosses starting just below the top of the stem and continuing in a straight line to the right suggest serenity and largeness of spirit.

Finally, in precise script (see page 41), the cross through the 't' will be careful and studied, in harmony with the overall context of the script, although sometimes it can be very ostentatious, as if it were an escape from the constrictions in which the individual is forced to live.

This series of examples shows that the cross through the 't', while of considerable value in establishing charac-ter through handwriting, cannot be considered separately from the overall context of the graphological signs of which it forms a part. Indeed, even the most careful graphologist will fail to grasp the precise significance of the fleeting gesture if he does not consider it in conjunction with other signs that confirm and support its characteristics.

The length and thickness of the stroke do not signify the time it took to produce the cross as this is a fleeting gesture which the writer makes by impulse.

### Long 't' cross

The 't' cross is measured in relation to the size of the ovals and spaces between the letters: a cross is defined as long if its extension exceeds the horizontal dimensional of a loop and a space between letters – it can measure as much as six ovals.

*'T' crosses are one of the most easily recognized graphological signs*

People with a long 't' cross face up to the events of life with enthusiam. They have sufficient audacity not to be outfaced by difficulties, although they are quite likely to get excited about a cause which subsequently proves to be not worth the effort used to sustain it. These are individuals liable to have outbursts of anger in which they are unable to control what they say. They have a high level of aggression, which may be a positive trait if it is channelled in involvement and determination, but can also be nega-tive at times of anger and irritation. Those in question tend to assume roles of command which they exercise im-periously and arrogantly. They have no inhibitions and abandon themselves to their desires, which often lead them into hazardous enterprises.

## Short 't' cross

Short 't' crosses are those that do not exceed the width of one oval; they denote immobility of ideas in the face of obstacles, memory blocks at times of crisis and an inability to take decisive action in complex or difficult situations.

In terms of the emotions, they indicate an inability to express anger or displeasure, a tendency to idealize the loved one and difficulty in getting through emotional crises and in the relationship as a whole.

Subjects with this sign are inclined to have a stable emotional life, providing them with the security of those who need to avoid crises. They have no flights of passion, and their lives are thus devoid of impulse; they always follow the safe path that they know. They allow themselves to be intimidated by the presence of those whom they regard as their superiors, and are unable to function well in such circumstances. They are scrupulous in their undertakings, to the extent that they are terrified of being unable to see them through. They could never assume any role of management or command, as they are always uncertain and hesitant when faced with any choice, however trivial.

*A short 't' cross denotes an uncertain and indecisive nature*

## Thick 't' cross

Thick 't' crosses denote a tendency to command and to crush other people's ideas and feelings. The intensity of this sign is dictated by the thickness of the crosses. Writers of thick 't' crosses tend to distort reality and to see it from a totally subjective viewpoint. They also have many prejudices and tend to over-estimate themselves. They are adventurous but lack self-criticism and find it difficult to admit that they have made a mistake. When angry they are very harsh with others and will not tolerate disobedience.

## Thin 't' cross

In contrast to those with a thick 't' cross individuals with this sign show considerable delicacy in the way in which they advance their beliefs, but they are also weak-willed and show excessive respect for others, both in public and in private. They are always frightened of clashing with others or of offending others' sensibilities, and they repress their feelings to such an extent that tension builds up and they bear grudges that could easily be avoided. A thick 't' cross will be difficult to detect if the script being examined has been written in ball point pen. It is best always to try and obtain samples which have been written with a fountain pen in ink.

## Thickening 't' cross

Thickening 't' crosses are those that become thicker towards the right. The percentage is calculated on the basis of the frequency with which this occurs. This sign denotes a writer who, while having the ambition to command, acts cautiously, and before exposing himself or herself to risk will consider the surrounding circumstances. However, he or she becomes irritated if anything or anyone places obstacles in his or her way, preventing him or her from dominating the situation.

## Thinning 't' cross

Crosses are described as thinning when the stroke becomes thinner as it proceeds towards the right. This sign is typical of hypersensitive individuals who allow themselves to be conditioned by external events. Such people will quickly abandon their ideas when faced with obstacles. Thinning crosses are generally found in handwriting that also exhibits thinning stems.

## Incorporated 't' cross

Incorporated crosses indicate extreme practicality. People with this sign are also endowed with considerable ingenuity and are swift in their deductions, decisions and choices. Highly impatient, they get angry if crossed. Their excessive practical sense may have a negative effect on their actions and intentions.

## Repeated 't' cross

Repeated 't' crosses – those made twice or even three times – denote a wish for clarity. Their percentage occurrence is calculated by evaluating their frequency – usually there are very few.

Those with this sign need very clear teaching, are unable to avoid repeating themselves, ponder over decisions that they have already taken and tend to criticize themselves exaggeratedly, always being ready to go over again anything that relates to them. Emotionally they are tense and liable to suffer frequent feelings of guilt and remorse, which are often unjustified.

## Robert Taylor

Another famous American film star was Robert Taylor, who was born in Nebraska in 1911. Tall, handsome, and charming, he gained his first successes towards the middle of the thirties. He appeared dozens of times in costume dramas and action films, showing himself to have a perfect mastery of cinema techniques. Taylor's autograph is signed in haste, with a right to left underline and an extended capital 'T' cross. This signals a passionate, impetuous nature.

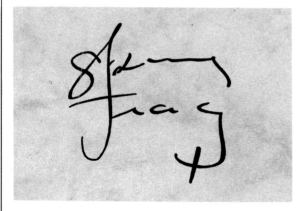

## Spencer Tracy

Spencer Tracy was born in Wisconsin in 1900. In 1922, he registered with the American Adacemy of Dramatic Arts in New York. He won an Oscar for *Captain Courageous* in 1937 and his career continued till he became one of the most popular and best-loved stars in Hollywood. At the beginning of the thirties a romantic love story, destined to continue for 25 years, began between Tracy and Katharine Hepburn. His signature exhibits a number of embellishments, including a relatively long crossbar on the capital 'T'.

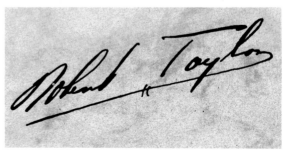

# Upstrokes and downstrokes

A highly significant graphological sign, and one that is easy to identify and evaluate, is that of the upper and lower extensions of letters such as d, f, g, h, l, p. q and t. These are known as the upstrokes and downstrokes.

In the field of graphology there are three distinct zones: the body of the letter, which represents the zone of self; the upper extensions, which represent the zone of ideals; and the lower extensions, which represent the zone of instincts.

The unit of measurement for extensions is based on the dimension of the body of the letter – more precisely on the ovals.

In the letter 'g' shown below, the lower extension is two ovals in length, while in the letter 'd' shown beside it, the upper extension is of the same length as its oval.

## Balanced extensions
The extensions are in proportion to the body of the words when their length is equal to two superimposed ovals. This means that the self (the horizontal part) is balanced with the intellect (the upper extensions) and the instincts (the lower extensions).

In this case, the writers are sufficiently self-aware to be able to control their idealistic and instinctive impulses. They therefore live in harmony in the relationship between their own and external reality; they understand their own limitations and do not squander their energies in projects that they know they will be unable to see through.

*Balanced extensions speak for a well-balanced personality*

## Short upper and lower extensions
Where upper and lower projections are very short this indicates a lack or total absence of the idealistic impulses that help an individual to extend himself or herself and try out new ground. This applies to both cultural curiosity and to material possessions. At a time when science is advancing every day and the products of new technology are within everyone's reach, the writer feels less and less motivated to be a protagonist, and clings to the past. He or she flees from anything and prefers to anchor himself or herself to the familiar, depicting his or her situation with handwriting that is flattened out and devoid of peaks.

## Long upper and lower extensions
When both the lower and upper extensions are excessive writers exhibit two opposing forces of equal strength, one pushing them into the area of ideals and the other into that of instinct. They are thus torn between these two opposing tendencies and are liable to venture into far-reaching projects which they are unable to carry through because they lack a balanced grasp of reality.

*A writer with long upper and lower extensions is unrealistic*

## Long upper extensions
Excessively long upper extensions indicate a dominance of the zone of ideals. This writer has a distorted view of reality and his or her instincts are ignored as his or her feelings are experienced mainly in the imagination.

*Long upper extensions reflect an idealistic mind*

## Long lower extensions
When the lower extensions are excessive the writer has insufficient self-control and tends to waste his energies in activities to which he is not suited. Living primarily at instinctive level, his interests are in material pleasures.

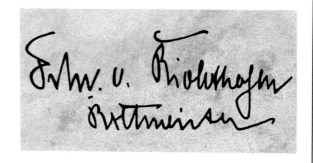

There is a curious affinity linking these two figures who in other respects were quite different from one another: a shared passion for flying, a love of danger and intense competitiveness.

An examination of the signatures of Baron Manfred von Richthofen, legendary German flying ace in the First World War, and Colonel Charles A. Lindbergh, hero of the first flight across the Atlantic, finds in both, through the emphasis of the upper extensions, the quest for greatness and for new limits against which to test their abilities.

## Charles Lindbergh

Charles Lindbergh was born in 1902 and began work as a pilot in the government air service in 1925. He is famous for making a record transatlantic flight in *The Spirit of St Louis*, when he travelled from New York to Paris in 33 hours.

The more restrained proportions and, in particular, the closeness of the letters in the American aviator's name, show a tendency to withdraw into himself.

## Baron Manfred von Richthofen

Baron Manfred von Richthofen was born in 1892. He was commander during World War 1 of the 11th Chasing Squadron (*Richthofen's Flying Circus*). He was shot down in 1918, after being credited with 80 air victories. The presence of flourishes and roundness in the handwriting of the audacious German pilot, nicknamed the 'Red Baron' because of the colour he had his plane painted, clearly indicates exhibitionism.

*A painting from the ancient Roman city of Pompeii, now housed in the National Museum, Naples*

# Dotting the 'i's

The dot over the letter 'i' is regarded as a fleeting gesture, with everything that this entails. This sign differs considerably between writers and bears witness to a number of basic characteristics of the writer's personality, very often in relation to his mood. It is, of course, considered within the whole complex range of signs in a particular handwriting, since it would be of little significance if taken alone.

## High dot

If the dots over the 'i' are placed more than halfway up the upper extension they are considered to be high. This sign indicates a tendency to magnify even the tiniest details and so lose sight of the central core of the problem. These writers dwell on unimportant matters, and thus dissipate their energy, attention and mental lucidity.

They are governed in their social and emotional relationships by the difficulty that they experience in taking a realistic view. They show themselves to be incapable of understanding others and have an idealized image of the person they love.

## Low dot

Anyone with the sign of a low dot over the 'i' is liable to be over-concerned with strictly material matters, to the detriment of honesty and morality. A preoccupation with acquiring material assets leads such writers to disregard the means used to attain their objectives. They will be grudging when it comes to sharing out material goods.

## Centred dot

A precisely centred dot over the 'i' indicates fastidiousness; these people are over-precise and waste energy and resources by paying undue attention to details that could easily be disregarded. They concern themselves with clarifying specific details and their ability to· assimilate ideas suffers as a result. They are lacking in practicality and are slow to act, their actions always being hampered by wasted time. They lack originality and tend to repeat themselves as a result of their constant need to check and take stock. They move around their environment slowly, lacking in speed and initiative. In terms of feelings, they suffer from inhibitions, excessive control of their emotions and a lack of warmth. People with this sign lack spontaneity and do not enjoy the pleasures of good living.

## Displaced to the right

A dot over the 'i' that is displaced to the right is the result of haste. The maximum degree applies when the dot is as much as two letters and two spaces ahead of the 'i'.

Anyone with this sign has a tendency to act hastily, with correspondingly reduced attention to detail, and they can lack the ability to concentrate over long periods of time. However, the writer has a dynamic personality and a considerable ability to absorb concepts quickly and act upon them with equal speed. If, in rushing into things, this person misses important details, he or she is often sufficiently practical to see a way around any resulting problems.

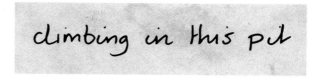

*A dot displaced to the right of the 'i' suggests haste*

## Connected dot

If a dot is placed well away from the 'i', this means that the pen has been lifted after making the stroke. When this phase has been eliminated and the dot is connected to the stroke this indicates not only practicality but also a good deal of ingenuity. Connected dots denote a capacity for logic, a practical approach and consistency of thought.

## Dash-like dot

Dash-like dots denote a considerable amount of anxiety. Those with this sign have good powers of concentration and learning. They have a pronounced sense of responsibility, and confront life with a certain trepidation due to their need for correctness and precision.

## Circle dot

Circle dots over the 'i' denote an obsession with clarity and and a preoccupation with trivial details to the detriment of making reasoned decisions. As far as the emotions are concerned, circle dots denote stubbornness, nervousness and fussiness, and someone who tends to quibble and pay undue attention to trivial matters. The writer has a childish or immature, irresponsible mentality.

## Dots omitted

Finally, the dot over the 'i' may be totally omitted; this sign denotes carelessness, negligence, and a poor memory. This writer will be vague, imprecise and hesitant when making decisions. He or she does not assess the importance of certain details, and consequently pays little attention to any form of detail.

H·G·WELLS· · 1919 ·

H. G. Wells

R.J. SWAN, 1919

# 3

# Personality Traits

Is your handwriting all the same size – or do certain letters loom large in comparison to the rest? A visually pleasing difference in size is the sign of systematic inequality, and it signifies originality, creativity, talent and intuition. If you are going to be a good graphologist your writing will almost certainly have this sign. If, however, the disparity between the letters is also accompanied by irregularity in the thickness of the strokes and by fits and starts, this augurs badly for success in handwriting analysis, as it is a sign of someone who is inconsistent and who fails to link elements together to gain an overall view.

Meticulous handwriting reveals just what you might expect – a tendency towards precise reproduction without any originality. Such a person will always stick to routine and will not enjoy change; his dress, his speech, his manners and his menus all have to be just so.

The sign of speed is the most indicative of how fast the brain works. People who think quickly have difficulty in writing swiftly enough to keep up with their thoughts and their handwriting demonstrates this.

All of these signs, of course, have their opposites, and their intensity governs how much weight they carry in the final analysis of all the different aspects of the writing. In this chapter some striking traits of personality manifested in handwriting are analysed, with examples.

*A portrait of H. G. Wells, the famous science fiction writer, by R. J. Swan, 1919*

# Original and brilliant

What do the letters of handwriting look like when they are compared with one another – is the overall effect harmonious or disharmonious? In both adults and the very young correct observation of this sign provides valuable information. A difference in the size of the letters can indicate both originality or disorganization, depending on whether or not the disparity between the letters is in proportion and in harmony.

When learning to write a child is taught to copy a standard model, using suitably lined paper. Then, as he or she becomes more skilled, he or she makes his or her own variations to the model to suit his or her need for originality. Even small children, however, may fail to keep to the same size: this implies a lack of willpower, but also denotes an ability to make their own personal response.

There are a number of aspects relating to handwriting of uniform size. It denotes strength of will and accuracy as well as monotony and conventionality. Handwriting that increases or decreases progressively in size, on the other hand, is indicative of weak willpower. The writer is unable to control impulses and desires adequately.

## Systematic inequality

When the handwriting exhibits harmonious – that is, compositionally pleasing – differences in the size of the letters, this is the graphological sign of systematic inequality. The intensity of the sign increases the more perceptible, as well as harmonious, the inequality between the letters becomes. It should also be added that the inequalities, even if less obvious, are more significant in

small handwriting and that as the size of the writing increases the relevance of the intensity of the sign decreases. The differences should not be considered individually, but only if they occur with some frequency in two or three lines of the text.

Systematic inequality is significant in the field of intelligence: it indicates originality, creativity, imagination, clear-sightedness, talent, brilliance, intuition. Those with this sign reveal a unique personality, especially relevant in the field of the arts. They detest repetition and are always looking for change and for new horizons. They show originality even when they take over ideas from others by reworking them in their own style.

As a rule, the sign is indicative of a novel way of life. It must always be interpreted in the context of the handwriting as a whole, and it primarily modifies other signs and adds originality and flair to their meaning.

Systematic inequality combined with height denotes organizational skills and a clear perception of goals to be achieved using suitable means without paying too much attention to detail. With broad spacing between words and medium size, the sign denotes a leaning towards scientific research.

> Moral: Buy yourself a pair of sunglasses.

*Harmonious writing with different sized letters shows artistic flair*

The systematic inequality sign has innate characteristics of brilliance and originality that take on a positive or negative aspect according to whether they are accompanied by positive or negative characteristics expressed by other signs. If the originality and brilliance are used in a spirit of good will and generosity they signify creativity and the ability to coordinate other people's activities: if, on the other hand, they are used with insincerity and disloyalty, they give rise to deceit and underhandedness.

Finally, people who have the sign of systematic inequality are free spirits, always seeking new means of expression. In order for them not to withdraw into themselves, feeling they are misunderstood, they must always know how and in which direction to channel their unceasing flow of ideas.

A child with this sign should be understood and supported in his or her effervescent spirit:

*Two brilliant scientists: above is a painting of Louis Pasteur and to the right a portrait of Alexander Fleming*

## Pasteur and Fleming

Imagination, self-confidence, open-mindedness and an uncheckable curiosity: these are the ingredients that are unquestionably to be found in the personalities of great scientists and researchers. The right hand slope and fullness in the signatures of Pasteur and Fleming bear witness to these qualities; such qualities are essential to making the discoveries that represent a great stride forward in man's scientific knowledge.

# Impulsive and disorganized

The harmonious relationship between the component elements of handwriting, and indeed of any graphic, pictorial or musical composition, indicates the way in which an author relates to the people and things habitually around him or her. Someone who expresses themselves graphically through harmoniously matched strokes, for example, will undoubtedly have a balanced attitude to life.

The equality between the size of various letters making up the words is not necessarily the same as a harmoniously matched relationship. When the difference between the letters is systematic and orderly, this endows the handwriting with grace and denotes a series of extremely positive characteristics illustrated by the graphological sign of systematic inequality. Contrastingly, unequal letter sizes and spacing and stopping and starting characterize disorderly handwriting.

## Disorderly handwriting

When the inequality in the size of the letters applies in conjunction with fits and starts and sudden thinning of the stroke, the graphological sign exemplified is disorderliness. Its distinctive feature is a lack of proportion between the various elements of the handwriting.

There are no real parameters for evaluating the intensity of the sign: you should therefore restrict yourself to ascertaining whether the disorderliness is present in the whole of the handwriting, in part of it, or only sporadically. In all cases, the greater the disorderliness the more accentuated the intensity of the sign.

In terms of the intellect, the sign indicates muddled thinking and feelings and disorderliness in the writers' ideas and intentions. Those with a high level of disorderliness, while on the one hand having minds that are teeming with ideas and plans, on the other lack the organization necessary to put their proposed initiatives into operation. The writers may waver between one concept and another, neglecting to do anything consistently.

In addition these writers will fail to take account of form, style and precision in their use of language. They will have a mass of ideas in their minds, which they will blurt out in a rush, but they will fail to link events together to gain an overall picture. They will also make thoughtless remarks without considering the potential consequences of their statements.

They are generally absent-minded, with poor memories, but are always ready to follow up new ideas, new sensations and new projects. The distinctive features of their mentalities are inconstancy, restlessness and agitation. They will act with an impulsiveness that they are unable to control, and they are unable to foresee the possible consequences of their actions. They are people who, failing to plan their work, tend always to act in response to sudden demands. Punctuality is not their strong point and they are fickle in their interests, affections and desires.

These writers can perform any activity or role even if it undermines their dignity. They lack a sense of values and tend to heed their instincts and impulses.

People who are disorderly in their minds are often the same in their appearance. The individuals in question pay little attention to their physical appearance, are untidy in their dress and they can even be uncoordinated in their movements. Their speech is usually incoherent, as they find it difficult to follow through their reasoning in an organized and concise fashion. They are generally inconsistent and may make statements that are based on momentary enthusiasm rather than on careful thought.

This is an overall picture of the characteristics relating to the graphological sign of disorderly handwriting and only applies to writing that exhibits a high level of intensity of the sign. When analysing handwriting you must evaluate the extent of the disorderly sign and from this deduce the relative level of organization of the individual's thoughts.

At school, a child with disorderly handwriting should be encouraged to focus his or her attention on one simple project at a time and to see it through to the end. He or she should be shown the comparisons between similar objects and events, in order to see how like objects and occurrences may be grouped.

*Disorderly handwriting indicates muddled thinking*

# Conformist and unimaginative

Conformist and unimaginative personalities are usually revealed in handwriting which is either naturally neat or very deliberately made to look neat with a resulting affectation of style.

## Meticulousness
Uniformity of size, direction, width of letters and spacing between letters and words is the distinctive feature of meticulous handwriting.

When the handwriting appears to have been reproduced to a rigid model to such an extent that it looks like printing, the sign is at maximum intensity. As the size and direction vary, so the intensity of the sign decreases.

*Neat handwriting is often the work of an unimaginative mind*

In the spheres of intelligence and willpower, the sign of meticulousness denotes a tendency towards precise reproduction with no personal input and devoid of any originality. In the case of handwriting with equal dimensions, the reproduction is mechanical but still spontaneous; in pedantic handwriting, on the other hand, the model is reproduced in an affected and obsessively meticulous manner. In both cases the common, most important element is the absolute absence of any personal touch which is typical of flat, predominantly repetitive intellectual activity.

People with the sign of meticulousness register ideas and concepts in their minds and retain them unchanged. They faithfully repeat what they have learned, tend always to work using the same methods, adhere strictly to set rules, and, even if events and general conditions should change, they will not alter their programmes. Their intellectual activity follows a totally methodical pace, devoid of impulsiveness and originality of any kind. Rushes of enthusiasm and flashes of brilliance are alien to their nature. Precise in their style and mindful of form, they express themselves in stereotyped language which is devoid of any passion or imagination: what they say must always be appropriate and exact.

Writers with the sign of meticulousness will tend to observe rigid rules of life. They are sticklers for routine, which they methodically carry out, and experience considerable difficulty in the face of change, particularly when the change is to be only temporary. They love traditions and strictly abide by them; they always follow the rules of the game and are punctual and require others to be the same. They cannot bear others' wishes to deviate from the norm, to the extent that they become repressive in relation to those close to them. They tend to impose their rules for living on others and cannot understand other people's aspirations.

These people are also narrow-minded and make plans on the basis of their past experience, which they regard as more valid than anyone elses. Overall, they place too much faith in their own abilities. Their choice of food, places to visit and clothing is affected, and they prefer that which is reputed to be the best without asking themselves why.

Over-refined in their manners, speech, dress, deportment and table manners, these people are highly satisfied when others notice what they regard as their essential qualities. They are permanently concerned with making a good impression and anxious to appear able to cope with situations at all times.

The sign of meticulousness may have the variables of both equality and pedantry: in the latter case, in addition to the traits already described, there is a total lack of spontaneity and warmth on the part of writers. Their gestures, which are controlled to the utmost, reveal the absence of mental elasticity typical of those who run away from innovation of any kind without even considering the challenge. This results in excessive rigidity, which they find difficult to control in their relations with others and, not least, in themselves.

These remarks, of course, apply only if the signs of meticulousness, equality or pedantry are found at an excessive level of intensity. When the sign is present to a lesser extent it merely signifies a tendency towards mechanical and impersonal reproduction, but it does not mean that this is the predominant characteristic.

Children who show a high percentage of the sign in their handwriting should be encouraged to experiment with the unknown, to examine facts carefully and to express themselves in a personal and original manner. With this in mind, it is useful to provide them with experiences that are rich in creative stimuli.

# Coherent or confused?

While a child is learning to write, he or she will learn to trace the letters following a strict model. As his or her independence of expression and his or her personal ability to communicate develop, these letters will increasingly become an expression of what he or she feels within himself or herself. The child no longer blindly follows the outline of the letters, but writes them in his or her own way under the influence of inner impulses of varying strength, using imagination and creativity.

Moving on from children to adults, if individuals are able to see themselves, clearly, they will be able to reproduce the structure of letters in their handwriting. If they are confused and uncertain the outline of the letters will reflect this. Muddled thought processes are reflected in such handwriting, because handwriting is a spontaneous manifestation of the character of a person.

Serene, lucid thought is reflected in the clarity of the way in which the letters are formed. In clear handwriting the hand receives calm, controlled messages and will produce a placid style. If, on the other hand, the writer's thoughts are confused and tumultuous, agitated messages will be transmitted to his or her hands, producing handwriting in which the forms are ill-defined; the writer fails to take account of space, distances and of all elements that provide order and proportion.

Tangles and knots may be found around certain letters; these indicate a focusing of attention on individual facts by someone who lacks an overall view of reality. More frequently, however, the handwriting follows a relatively regular course. This is the sign of clear handwriting.

### Clear handwriting
The maximum intensity of the sign applies when all the letters are clearly legible: if 90 per cent are clear, it applies to a level of 9/10, and so on.

Clarity, in terms of intelligence, means discernment and the habit on the part of the writers of expressing themselves in appropriate language. People with this sign show clarity in everything that they say, both in their language and in the precise concepts which they express. They attach great importance to stating their views, which they have reached with lucidity of thought.

Carelessness of any kind being quite alien to their natures, they cannot bear disorder and confusion and will tend to keep their surroundings in a state of tidiness. They are fastidious about their personal hygiene, attributing considerable significance to it on grounds not of appearance but of its importance in their lives.

Those with the sign of clarity will become intensely emotionally involved and will show their feelings spontaneously. They cannot bear, and would never indulge in, insincerity or deceit. People like this might appear a little cold and calculating, but they are unquestionably reliable and honest. They would make excellent teachers given the clarity with which they present things and the precision of their explanations.

*Clear, well-formed letters suggest an open, honest temperament*

### Obscure handwriting
The opposite to clear handwriting is obscure handwriting. This is so defined when the letters are hard to read. In establishing its intensity, the same rules apply as in clear handwriting. As the two signs are mutually exclusive, the amount of obscurity is complementary to the amount of clarity: in handwriting with 6/10 obscurity the remaining 4/10 will be attributable to the sign of clarity.

In terms of intelligence, the sign of obscurity denotes incoherence and vagueness. Even though a person with this sign may have good intellectual abilities, he or she has difficulty in expressing himself or herself and in organizing his or her thoughts, so that his or her performance is not in line with his or her abilities.

These writers will tend towards approximation rather than clarifying or detailing their opinions. Their behaviour is ambiguous both in their love lives and in relation to the people around them. Their inability to express themselves clearly often causes them to feel isolated, and they lack confidence with other people. They may, however, succeed in demonstrating through their actions what they are unable to explain in words.

If the sign of obscurity is found only to a limited extent in the handwriting the difficulties that it involves may be attenuated by other signs that are characteristic of opposite tendencies. If the sign of obscurity is present to a substantial degree in a child's handwriting, the child should be given clear guidelines and detailed answers to his or her questions to alleviate mental confusion.

# Quick or slow thinking?

In writing, you externalize inner energies at a rate that is congenial to your character, behaviour and emotions. The faster your mental processes, the faster your graphic tempo. Alternatively if the mind is slow, so is the graphic rhythm.

The sign of speed may be used to define writing that is formed quickly and without stopping. This sign is reinforced by letters of constant height and breadth, particularly when the letters are small. When all of these features apply, the sign has an intensity of 10/10: this is reduced if any of the above requirements are missing. If the percentage drops to below 50, the sign of speed no longer applies, being replaced by its opposite, slowness.

## Speed
Speed, in relation to willpower and intelligence, denotes general quickness of behaviour, disregard for detail and a tendency to draw conclusions quickly. People who have this sign have innate swiftness of thought and show spontaneity and a ready wit.

*Letters of similar height and breadth define speedy writing*

They are consistent in their decisions, which they make quickly without pondering on facts of minor importance. They have considerable energy and will always be where there is action. If they find themselves compelled to work under people whose tempo is slow they feel resentment and may lose their temper, albeit only momentarily.

Writers with the sign of speed always want to complete things quickly; they eat, walk, gesticulate and talk fast. They are not great lovers of civilities and respect only those rules that are essential in social life.

Those with speedy writing will succeed in life because they are able to act promptly, undertake new ventures, pick themselves up quickly from misfortune and always somehow see things through to the end. They speak fluently and effectively and always appear to be pleasant.

When the rapidity becomes of the neurotic type, of course, the positive values expressed by the sign of speed are negated by excessive hastiness which can easily lead

to mistakes. A child who writes quickly should be encouraged in his or her desire to do things, but take care to prevent his or her haste from rendering him or her superficial.

## Slowness
The graphological sign of slowness is the opposite to that of speed. Slowness applies when the writing is sluggish and sedate. If the handwriting is slow because of meticulousness it becomes precise, but it may be slow from lack of attention to the task in hand.

To measure the percentage intensity of the sign, the presence of other signs that exclude speed should also be assessed. For example, when the sign of dynamism (see page 44) is missing and when spacing between words is virtually non-existent, slowness applies at a rate of 10/10.

In the fields of intelligence and willpower, the sign of slowness denotes sluggishness in grasping concepts, processing data and taking action. Subjects with this sign will

*Slow, sluggish handwriting reveals a similarly slow temperament*

tend to move languidly, will have difficulty in learning and will not always succeed in reaching the right conclusions. They will be uneasy when faced with new problems and slow in completing tasks that they have undertaken. They will not be good at sizing up a situation and will tend to perform roles of secondary importance so they are not forced to commit themselves to big decisions.

In gestures, too, the sign indicates sluggishness, lethargy and listlessness. It is characteristic of people who are slow by nature, and anything that they do they will do unenthusiastically and after lengthy deliberation. They are often ineffectual and somewhat unreliable.

Care needs to be taken, however, to assess the percentage of the sign correctly – if its incidence is only marginal it does not indicate such a negative picture as that described. A child with a high percentage of the sign should be pushed and encouraged to prevent his or her tendency towards laziness from becoming a real defect.

# Decisive or hesitant?

Two opposing types of writing, dynamic and wavering, indicate personalities which are either consistent and quick at taking decisions or insecure and dependent on others.

### Dynamic handwriting
The sign of dynamism applies when handwriting has spirally linked letters or letters that are cut off cleanly, with fast, fleeting strokes. The maximum intensity of dynamism applies when this appears in all of the letters: if its incidence is 90, 80 or 70 per cent, this gives $9/10$, $8/10$ and $7/10$ intensity respectively.

In terms of intelligence and willpower, dynamism denotes unceasing, feverish activity of thought and action. Persons with this sign will learn extremely fast and will quickly draw conclusions, not pondering at length but weighing things up swiftly. In planning their work they do not dwell on details; their style is to be simple, plain and easily understood. In carrying out a project they are tense and anxious lest it should go wrong.

*Dynamic handwriting distinguished by fast fleeting strokes*

They are thrifty in their use of resources and quick in every way – in their speech, their actions, their calculations and so on. They dislike ceremony of any kind, and establish straightforward relationships with others. Their language is clear, they are never long-winded, and they prefer an immediate, incisive type of communication. They tend to repress their anger but when they lose their temper they explode in brief outbursts from which they quickly recover.

Those with this sign are intolerant of obstacles which stand in their way of doing things. They dislike duplicity or falsehood; they will never go back on their word and their enterprise and candour make them pleasant individuals.

In their love lives they are sincere and loyal. In terms of aptitude, they are ideally suited to work that requires flexibility and leaves room for initiative.

These writers are always ready to shoulder their responsibilities. With robust physiques and strong muscles, they will readily respond to external stress from which they draw stimulation and ideas for new undertakings. Their gestures are ever-changing and dynamic and they have a lively, attentive look and a firm, natural manner.

### Wavering
The sign of wavering applies when the direction of the letters varies in groups, so that one group of letters leans to the right, another to the left, and yet another is upright. It includes differences in the direction of the stroke.

Maximum intensity applies when the phenomenon is present in every word. If it affects 90, 80 or 70 per cent, then the sign applies with an intensity of $9/10$, $8/10$ and $7/10$ respectively. Wavering does not exist at a percentage of less than 50, as it is then defined as hesitancy.

In terms of willpower, the sign denotes a tendency towards indecisiveness, difficulty in completing things, limited spontaneity, uncertainty of judgement and general instability.

People with this sign suffer from insecurity in all their undertakings. They experience considerable embarrassment and awkwardness when required to take decisions, even when these are of minor significance. Any obstacles or difficulties cause them dismay and will result in their abandoning projects or activities. They remain disoriented in the face of anything new, will fail to occupy management roles, and are unable to maintain their views with sufficient conviction. Indecision, uncertainty and hesitancy are the reasons for their relative lack of success, with a resultant frustration and loss of faith in their own abilities and potential.

Those who write like this are not sufficiently mature and independent and tend to rely on others for support, from whom they seek assistance in making decisions and at times of difficulty. This dependence is often ill-judged, causing them to fall victim to somewhat undesirable characters who do not hesitate to use them. When the slant is fluctuating it also means that the subjects' logical and rational deductions frequently conflict with their emotionally-based decisions. Consequently their moods are changeable and because of their indecisiveness they often alter their plans and objectives.

With their inability to analyse the various aspects of a problem, they never manage to acquire an objective view of reality. In terms of their career, they suffer from continuous uncertainty which has an adverse effect on the success of their activities. They can work on simple tasks that require no initiative or responsibility, but to perform a job with even the slightest degree of confidence they need guidance in the tiniest details so that they can restrict themselves simply to carrying out the material task in hand.

People with this sign are awkward in their movements, underlining their emotional and psychological condition. They generally have a low opinion of themselves, they are hesitant in their stride, they will avert their eyes from others, they have a stiff and rigid physique and their speech is stilted and lacking in incisiveness.

These are, of course, the characteristics of individuals with a very high percentage of this sign. More often it is present to a lesser degree, and then it merely denotes a slight tendency to avoid responsibility and to occupy roles which are not demanding in terms of the decisions these writers may have to cope with on their own.

A child with wavering handwriting should be encouraged to accept responsibility so as to gain confidence in his or her own potential.

*Ancient Egyptian hieroglyphics carved into a statue of the god, Thoth*

# Courteous and refined

The aesthetic element is extremely significant in character analysis through handwriting. It reveals not only what the person is really like, but also the image that he or she wishes to present to others.

The degree of affectation of letters or groups of letters indicate the writer's manner, his or her relations with others, his or her choice of dress and his or her use of language in expressing himself or herself in an elegant and courteous fashion. If, on the other hand, the writer is slovenly his or her handwriting will be careless.

## Polished handwriting

Handwriting in which excessive attention is paid to making it look elegant, where extremely light pressure has been used, which is of small, or at any rate less than medium, size and which has considerable fluidity, is described as polished. The sign applies to a degree of 10/10 if it is also devoid of frills and curls.

If all of these elements are present but there is little smoothness, the sign applies to a level of 8/10; if the size is medium, the maximum level will be 5/10–6/10. If the intensity of the sign falls to below 5/10, the sign of polish no longer applies and the handwriting should instead be defined as precise.

*Polished handwriting is the sign of an elegant disposition*

In terms of willpower and intelligence, the sign of polish denotes considerable competence and great courtesy, clarity of thought and expression and charm and gentleness in personal relationships; all of these characteristics are, however, veiled by a certain affectedness.

People with this sign will be careful in their way of thinking and acting and will never fail to be accurate and precise, although they will still remain lively and spontaneous. They are extremely thorough in their explanation of concepts, and express themselves with a suitable vocabulary.

The sign of polish indicates only a manner and a way of externalizing the intellectual abilities characteristic of other signs. Polished handwriting denotes a passion for methodology which never goes far enough to become meticulousness (see page 41).

Mentally, the sign indicates the same characteristics as precise handwriting, but to these it adds daintiness in behaviour and refinement in the feelings, and it omits the passion for organization revealed by precise handwriting. Persons with the sign of polish will succeed in adapting spontaneously and naturally to changing events and to any new situations that might arise. Highly accommodating types, they will not insist on their own views as they will seek to avoid possible attacks on their self-esteem. They do not like to be the loser or to be shown publicly to be in the wrong.

They are not shocked when faced with circumstances that do not really fit in with their own way of thinking – on the contrary, they appear to be extremely compliant to the extent even of being capable of lying.

Those with this sign will do anything to be noticed when they have to exhibit their work, which they will present with a wealth of detail using cultivated language. They will often pay excessive attention to style and ignore the essence of the matter; in addition, they assign too much importance to detail, running the risk of missing the point.

Emotionally, too, these people show a considerable degree of affectation, tending to idealize their romantic relationships rather than see them from a realistic perspective. Polish, together with other signs that denote emotional fragility, also implies a relative lack of sex drive.

They always use tact and diplomacy in dealing with others, and will flee from anything that seems to them to be coarse and vulgar. Lovers of good manners and of anything that enhances their appearance, they abhor violence, brutality and savagery.

People with this sign will be successful at jobs that require precision, accuracy and attention to detail. If the sign, which merely indicates method of approach, is supported by others that denote specific abilities with regard to flexibility, open-mindedness and intelligence in general, it may be indicative of a highly refined personality from all points of view.

Physically, people with the sign of polish are well-cared for and elegant in their appearance; they dress with taste, paying attention to detail, are soft and delicate in manner and particularly careful in their gestures, which are never violent or brusque.

A child who shows this sign in his or her handwriting should be gently taught to take the initiative and to be practical and realistic in his decisions, but his tastes for refinement and style should be respected since, if frustrated, this could cause him or her deep trauma, and even outright rejection of relations with other people.

## Rudolph Valentino

Rodolfo Valentino was born Rudolph Guglielmi at Castellaneta in Italy in 1895. He emigrated to America in search of work and was employed in a wide range of jobs before appearing in the cinema, almost by chance. *The Four Horsemen of the Apocalypse*, made in 1921, turned him into a star idolized by the public worldwide. Women fell madly in love with him and men imitated him. Those dark, Latin lover's eyes brought him devoted fans, and when he died at the age of only 31 their distress bordered on hysteria. His signature is clean, regular and elegant and reveals a refined nature.

## Greta Garbo

Greta Gustaffson, better known as Greta Garbo, was born in Stockholm on 18 September 1905. After studying at the Academy of Dramatic Art in her home city, she began her brief and luminous career in movies. She acted in Europe under the direction of such masters as Pabst and Stiller, but it was the 24 films produced in Hollywood from 1926 to 1941 that made her a legend. Greta Garbo was one of the greatest stars that has ever appeared on the screen, thanks to an ability to express herself with lyrical intensity and to convey the sufferings of thwarted love. When she suddenly made her irrevocable decision to abandon her career, she withdrew completely from the public eye, thus contributing to the legend that was attached to her name. Her films include *Flesh and the Devil*, *Mata Hari*, *Anna Karenina* and *Ninotchka*. Her precise, legible autograph, written with little pressure, reveals a shy and very attractive nature.

# Calm or impatient?

The rhythm of handwriting is governed by the inner impulses that we all contain to a greater or lesser degree. Intense mental activity is translated into complex, articulated gestures, just as a flat and monotonous mental outlook is manifested in slow, phlegmatic or simply disorganized writing.

Rhythm, more than anything else, indicates the individual's inner energy type: inner calm is shown by a correspondingly calm rhythm while nervous tension is betrayed by impatience in the handwriting.

## Calmness

Calmness is shown when the strokes are written, both horizontally and vertically, with no sudden breaks, when there is no difference in pressure, and no curls.

In the field of willpower, calmness denotes self-assurance, stability and regularity in the various aspects of life. People with this sign have good control over themselves, never act hastily and are able to weigh up the facts before satisfying their own impulses and instincts.

They are not worried by dangers or adversity and even if they suffer serious setbacks they always manage to pick themselves up again without losing heart. As they are basically well-balanced they do not allow themselves to be carried away by momentary enthusiasms or to be beaten down at difficult times. At work, they set themselves regular hours and a steady pace to avoid excessive fatigue or stress.

New sensations, sudden enthusiasms and sensational events fail to upset their equilibrium, as they have considerable self-control in response to innovations and changes. Nothing will distract them from completing the tasks that they have undertaken in accordance with their set objectives. This steadiness is not a sign of a cold or calculating nature but of a desire to understand before allowing themselves to be carried away by unforeseen events.

*Harvesting the vines is a slow process, as the pickers go through the vineyards*

*Horizontal and vertical strokes with no breaks denote calmness*

Although they succeed in maintaining a good level of self-control even in adverse circumstances, being sensitive individuals they may suffer increasing stress if a frustrating situation is frequently repeated.

From the intellectual point of view, calmness is not a determining factor. It is indicative of attitude, denoting an ability to take on work that requires self-control under complex circumstances, equitable judgement in the face of difficulties, punctuality with respect to deadlines and an honourable approach towards relationships.

People with the sign of calmness physically exhibit the characteristics described above through their steady gaze, controlled bearing and moderate gestures.

## Impatience

The antithesis of the graphological sign of calmness is that of impatience. This is typical of handwriting with clear words or characters which are often only sketchily written and sometimes totally omitted, as if the hand were writing under the influence of nervous tension and anxiety.

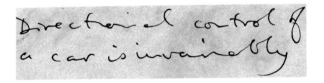

*Directional control of a car is invariably*

*Sketchy handwriting suggests impatience and a quick temper*

When these phenomena are present in every word the sign applies at a level of 10/10, while if they are found in 90, 80 or 70 per cent, the intensity is 9/10, 8/10 and 7/10 respectively. The incidence of impatience to an extent exceeding 7/10 denotes poor self-control, unstable psychological equilibrium and a quick temper. They will quickly reach a conclusion without first having considered the facts and will fail to take account of advice.

They rush into projects and find it difficult to stop and consider the pros and cons of them. They lack consistency, so that they will often abandon a project that they have begun in haste. They exhibit chaotic and relatively unproductive nervous energy and find it especially difficult to see through activities if they come across obstacles.

These people often change their plans, causing confusion to others. If the proportion of impatience signs is greater than 7/10, the individual suffers from a lack of balance, is easily disoriented and tends to be unreliable. This sign will always add a negative angle to the tendencies expressed by other signs.

Where the sign is found in a child's handwriting, while still young the child should be taught to think clearly and to develop self-control at difficult moments.

# Pompous and extravagant

Two types of handwriting, evident from adolescence onwards, reveal similar temperaments. They are known as solemn and arrogant handwriting, and a person with either of these types needs approval and recognition from others to be satisfied. A tendency to distort reality and to spend money like water are also common.

### Solemn handwriting
Stiffness and pomposity are fundamental elements of handwriting defined as solemn. This sign also applies when considerable pressure is exerted in the downstrokes, and if the signs of uprightness, a larger than medium size and at least a small percentage of precision are additionally present. The sign applies to a level of 10/10 if all of the above elements are found to the maximum extent: if present to a medium percentage it applies 5/10. Below this the sign ceases to exist.

In the field of the willpower, solemn handwriting denotes pomposity, ambition, rigidity in the affections, and desire for social elevation.

*Handwriting which is stiff and upright signifies ambition*

People with this sign are extremely aware of their personalities. They tend to draw attention to themselves, and have to succeed over others at all costs. Money is no object when it is a question of taking the lead, and they will always tend to occupy positions that enable them to ascend the social scale.

They demand absolute respect of their dignity and their considerable vanity means that they enjoy people's approval without stopping to consider whether what they say is genuine. They like to surround themselves with people that flatter them and constantly praise whatever they do.

They hold those in positions below their own in a state of subjection in order to feel that they are always the best in whatever they do. They are particularly fond of people who praise them without reservation even if their praise is false and unwarranted. They like to be the centre of attention and cannot stand indifference on the part of others, and become nervous and irritable if they believe that anyone is trying to put difficulties in their way. In their affections they are rigid and authoritarian, and they show no tenderness even to those dear to them.

People with the solemn sign are extremely conscious of style and form in every expression of their abilities. They are excellent at staging celebrations and receptions and show the best of themselves when they are anxious to make a good impression.

Physically, those with this sign are typically of solemn bearing with impressive physiques, sententious manners, authoritative voices and dignified expressions.

### Arrogant handwriting
The sign of arrogance is found when the letters, particularly the capitals, are over-showy, both in their large size and in their horizontal or vertical extension; overall, handwriting of this type creates an intrusive, bold impression.

The sign applies to a level of 10/10 when the capital letters are five or six times larger than the others, 7/10 when around four times larger and 6/10 when three times larger. Handwriting may be defined as arrogant, even if it is small in size, if the capitals are excessively large.

In terms of willpower, arrogance denotes a tendency towards megalomania, rudeness, invasion of other people's privacy, and of an inflated view of the writer's abilities.

Persons with this sign like to show off their achievements, plans and ambitions. They magnify themselves and denigrate others, tending to consider themselves to be the best.

They will invariably be optimistic, will take on commitments without considering whether or not they can cope with them, and are unscrupulous at all times, particularly when it is a matter of glorifying themselves. Money is no object when they are aiming at a particular goal as they are certain that they will succeed, and in the face of defeat they will tend to blame their failure on others.

In terms of their relationships, those with the sign of arrogance will have little depth as they will always tend to bolster their own megalomania, even if it means trampling on those around them; they are never prepared to put themselves second to satisfy other people's needs however important these may be.

Most of all they like the image of themselves that they put over to others, and they have little left to give to other people. They lack sincerity, are materialistic, and use those close to them as their public; relationships are sacrificed in their thirst for power. In terms of behaviour and appearance, the sign indicates arrogance, forwardness, superficiality and pushiness. People who write like this are generally undiscriminating in their choice of career, provided that they can increase their income.

# Disciplined and loyal

## Plain handwriting

The graphological sign of plain handwriting is the complete opposite of solemn and arrogant handwriting. It is found in handwriting which is devoid of curls or embellishments anywhere and is small in size.

To calculate the level of intensity of the sign you need to take into account both the size of the writing and the presence or otherwise of any curls. If the size is very small and there are no curls, maximum intensity may be assigned. When the size is medium with no curls, plainness applies to a level of 6/10. Below 5/10 the sign is insignificant.

People who have this sign like to be specific at all times, attributing due weight to things; they express concepts in concise form, and leave out minor details. They will not lose sight of the central core of a problem and will draw other people's attention to their ideas.

They succeed in attributing the correct importance and the right priority to things, avoiding confusion. At no time do they give free play to their imagination, always remaining within the limits of reality. They establish easy, uncomplicated relationships with others, and are unlikely to become involved in misunderstandings or disputes.

If the sign is accompanied by a certain percentage of precision, then the individuals in question are sober in their attitudes and cautious in their words and actions. They will not allow themselves to make promises unless they have first considered whether or not they will be able to keep them. They are composed, direct, loyal and consistent in their dealings with others.

The ability to weigh up facts and to think things over makes these people cautious and careful. They will only make a decision after thinking about it at length, but once they have decided they will adhere consistently to what they have assessed as being the best solution. They will flee from any form of foolhardiness or recklessness.

Every aspect of their characters is positively affected by their composure and fairness, and they appear to all to be respectable people in every sense, reliable in whatever they undertake to do, and with a marked sense of responsibility. Others have no hesitation in confiding their secrets to them, certain that they will be kept.

They have an iron morality and are objective in evaluating problems. Even in adversity they will maintain their customary composure. They are always moderate in their habits and never eat, drink or enjoy themselves to excess. Emotionally they are not effusive, but they demonstrate a capacity for lasting, responsible affection. In terms of their careers, subjects with the sign of plainness are destined for roles requiring responsibility.

## Self-moderation

Self-discipline primarily implies energy in connection with the willpower which expresses an extreme desire for order in the writers' personality. The characteristic features of such people are thus vigour and, at the same time, clarity; these will accordingly be found in handwriting in which, in spite of the force exerted, the letters retain the characteristics that distinguish them and do not deviate, save in small details, from the copybook style.

To evaluate the degree of self-discipline in handwriting, account has to be taken of the general context of the component signs. In the course of a predominantly dynamic, fluid style, for example, less value will be attributed to failure to respect the model in the reproduction of letters; in a slow, static style, on the other hand, diversification from the model assumes a more representative value.

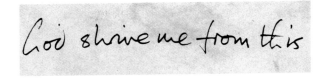

*Self-moderation, when letters are clearly written with speed*

The graphological sign of self-moderation is found to maximum intensity in highly fluid, fast-moving handwriting, but with no omission of the dots on the 'i's' or crosses on the 't's'. Those with this sign impose self-discipline on their actions. In terms of intelligence, they are endowed with clear ideas and concepts which they uphold vigorously; they succeed in getting to the crux of the matter through logic and clarity of vision.

People who write like this have considerable mental vigour, good organizational skills and are able to allot people and things to their rightful place. They quickly identify their goals and take decisions according to their own logically formed principles.

In their personal relationships these people know how to control their emotional urges, are loyal and straightforward in their amorous affairs and exercise control over their passions. Because they are self-disciplined, these people are unlikely to experience any inner conflict between mind and emotions. They are emotionally serene and are able to recover quickly from adversity.

Generally speaking, these people are able to explain themselves clearly and thoroughly and are highly efficient both in their work and in the use of their free time.

*An engraving of the great philosopher Immanuel Kant*

## Immanuel Kant

This eighteenth century German philosopher from Königsberg brought about a genuine speculative revolution, questioning in his *Critique of Pure Reason* all previous concepts of metaphysics. The philosophy of Kant provides a grandiose synthesis of fundamental trends in modern thought such as illuminism and empiricism. The *Critique*, Kant's major work, was published in 1781: it was a monument erected to the constitutional limits of the powers of reasoning. Kant was a fastidious man famous for his prevision: his autograph bears witness to rigid logical consistency.

*A portrait of Baruch Spinoza, the Dutch philosopher*

## Baruch Spinoza

Baruch Spinoza, the Dutch philosopher, was born on 24 November 1632 into a family of Portuguese Hebrews who had emigrated to the Netherlands to flee racial persecution. When he was 20 his unorthodox religious views led to his expulsion from the Jewish community in Holland. Spinoza's major work, the *Ethica*, was published after his death in 1677. It is divided into five parts, which are dedicated to God, to humanity, to passion, to the force of passion and to the power of the intellect. Ethics are demonstrated through geometric order, by a mathematical deductive process. The work concludes that liberty and necessity coincide in the contemplation of God and Nature.

Spinoza's signature is on the whole devoid of ornamentation. The capital 'B' is more elaborate but does not affect the basic style of the signature.

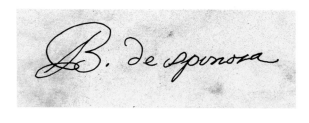

# 4

# Love

When you start to analyse handwriting, you will find that one of the most prevalent interests of your subjects will be their love life. It's part of human nature to want to know what we should look for in our lovers and what we should guard against in ourselves to save us from making unwise choices. Although some of the graphological signs do relate to love, none of them are exclusive of other factors concerning the character; for example, wide spacing between letters is found in someone optimistic and easily carried away by enthusiasms. Such people are ill-prepared to defend themselves against those who do not wish them well, and they are quite unable to see through people who have only a friendly demeanour. Although this applies to their life in general, it is easy to see that these people need to be committed to someone kind and loving before they get badly hurt. Narrow spacing between letters, on the other hand, is the sign of jealousy – that tormenting emotion which has ruined many a promising relationship.

As with all graphological signs, these give a useful pointer for the subject to understand where his problems lie and hence to take up the challenge of dealing with them; it is only when we really understand ourselves that we can begin to counter our undesirable features so as to make life run a little more smoothly!

*Portrait of Lady Hamilton, Lord Nelson's mistress, by George Romney, 1785 (see page 63)*

# Are you generous or envious?

The graphological sign of wide spacing between letters reveals the writers' capacity for projecting themselves on to the outside world and their ability to form well-balanced family relationships.

When we speak to another person we relate to them, giving them our attention to a greater or lesser extent depending on the degree of intimacy that we wish to establish with them. Their presence alters the way in which we would behave spontaneously.

In writing, on the other hand, the most significant fact is the unguarded way in which the writer's character is revealed. The writer, whenever he slants to the right, exhibits extroversion; and whenever he slants towards the left, he demonstrates inhibition. This principle always applies when you try to identify the writer's mental attitude towards the outside world.

## Wide spacing between letters

By judging the spacing between letters it is easy to infer the desire or otherwise on the part of writers to project themselves on the outside world.

The graphological sign of wide spacing between letters relates to the distance between one letter and the next. The unit of measurement is the oval of the 'a'. If it can be inserted between two letters, the sign applies at medium intensity of 5/10; if you can insert two units it applies to the maximum extent, 10/10. You can calculate intermediate levels by bearing in mind the principle that the space equivalent to an oval gives a level of 5/10.

When the 'wide spacing between letters' sign is approximately 6/10, this gives the optimum situation in which writers, without going too far, succeed in considering others and devoting due attention to them. They take a realistic view of life and do not allow themselves to be carried away either by undue optimism or undue pessimism. These writers tend, therefore, to assign things their correct importance. They are also able to put forward valid arguments to support their judgement of events and of people.

In addition, they are a source of good advice, because they are able to take an objective viewpoint. They have an ability to be generous when circumstances require; however, they can also be frugal when they decide that to spend money on any particular occasion would be wasteful.

Finally, those with 60 per cent of the sign show a very open mind to new ideas, which they accept after due consideration. The running of their households is always smoothly organized.

When the sign is present to a level exceeding 7/10, the individuals in question are over-generous to the extent of suppressing their own interests to satisfy those of other people. They are so optimistic and so easily carried away by enthusiasm that they are often ill-prepared for the results of their actions. They fail to protect themselves against ill-wishers, being unable to see through a friendly veneer. They are easily adaptable and feel no need for privacy.

## Narrow spacing between letters

Below 5/10, the graphological sign becomes narrow spacing between letters.

People with this sign tend to reject anything from other people and are closed in upon themselves. They have a narrow outlook and a tendency towards intellectual and mental meanness. Very often, envy and jealousy will prevent them from having a tranquil life and relaxed relationships.

*Example of average 5/10 spacing between letters*

A child who shows more than 7/10 wide spacing between letters may show a lack of prudence in his or her decision-making and is subject to danger in daily life, as he or she has a tendency towards optimism and is by nature naive.

A child whose writing shows less than 5/10 of the sign is also liable to present problems in view of his or her meanspirited behaviour towards others, whom he or she sees not as interesting people and potential friends but as objects of envy and jealousy who should be avoided whenever possible.

# Are you reasonable or emotional?

While excessive space between one letter and the next denotes too much generosity and a tendency towards wastage, letters that are too close together indicate oppression, in both the physical and the intellectual fields, with resultant difficulties in romantic relationships.

## Profusion

The graphological sign of profusion expands the significance of handwriting with wide spacing between letters. While someone who leaves a certain amount of space between one letter and the next demonstrates a good grasp of reality, someone who leaves too much space lacks a sense of proportion.

*Excessive letter spaces indicate a tendency to squander money*

At maximum intensity, when more than two ovals will fit between two letters, the sign denotes a tendency towards wastage in both intellectual and physical terms and excessive generosity, not out of a love of others but from an inability to hold on to things. While the characteristics of the sign of wide spacing between letters are such qualities as generosity and altruism, the sign of profusion turns these into defects. Generosity becomes a tendency to squander and altruism is taken to excess, to the detriment of the writer.

## Dilated handwriting

Further extension between two letters gives rise to the dilated handwriting sign, which further reinforces the negative characteristics of the sign of profusion. Here the handwriting has a number of small letters very close together or packed tightly against the preceding letters. This sign is usually combined with small handwriting with no extension of the top or bottom strokes.

People with this type of writing tend to be timid about showing their feelings or demonstrating their intellectual ability. They have considerable difficulty in their relationship with themselves and their relationships with other people. Although they are highly intelligent, they fail to take due advantage of their intelligence because they are always inhibited by their tense emotional situation. This deprives them of objectivity and sureness of judgement and action. The constant fear of making a mistake can render them sullen, sensitive and irritable. Their health is fragile as a result of their continuous state of anxiety which causes them to suffer from imaginary illnesses.

## Spacing between words

The sign of wide spacing between words relates to the distance between one word and the next, its intensity being judged from the average distance between the words. The regularity of these distances is also taken into account.

When eight round letters such as 'a' or 'o' could be inserted between one word and the next, the sign applies to a maximum degree of 10/10. When four letters could be inserted, it applies to a level of 5/10. Other levels are measured according to the same criterion.

A level of 5/10 of the graphological sign of wide spacing between words indicates an ability to see things as a whole. People with this sign show a preference for reason as opposed to emotional impulse: they have good powers of logic and show sufficient maturity in their use of it for intellectual analysis. They have a good critical sense and an aptitude for scientific research. Those who also have the sign of wide letters, which is an indication of depth of character, have attained a good level of wisdom.

*Word spacing at a level of 5/10 reflects a logical thinker*

Excessive spacing between words is symptomatic of a hypercritical nature, making these individuals rigid in their relationships and quibblers who are always ready to correct their own and other people's viewpoints.

Inadequate wide spacing between words is an indication of a poor critical sense, superficiality and limited commitment in terms of both willpower and intellect. Lack of space between the words is partly counteracted by small writing but aggravated by large handwriting.

# Inability to love

The connections between letters and sometimes between words are highly indicative elements in handwriting. Children are taught to connect their letters with visible, definite lines in reproducing the copybook style; they always join them up with care. Gradually the copybook style is abandoned and the handwriting takes on spontaneity, the connections becoming automatic, produced without thinking.

## Connected handwriting
Connected letters show a rhythm that is generated by cohesive thought, while handwriting with few connections denotes interruptions in the mental flow.

Handwriting may be defined as connected when the letters making up the words are written with no interruption in the stroke, and without the pen being lifted from the paper. Evaluation of the intensity of this sign is based on the frequency or otherwise of connections. In general, the sign will be found in conjunction with its opposite, and handwriting is defined as connected or disconnected according to the predominance of one or other of the signs.

Connected handwriting is typical of individuals who are able to take an overall view of events without dwelling on minor details. They are inclined to summarize, this tendency being further confirmed by the graphological sign of wide letters.

Connected handwriting indicates consistency, logic and coherence if supported by other signs that confirm these tendencies. When, on the other hand, it is found in conjunction with signs that denote superficiality (narrow spacing between words) or inconsiderateness (very wide spacing), connected handwriting represents the tendency on the part of the writers to follow their own logic despite the reality of the facts.

## Disconnected handwriting
When the stroke is broken, the graphological sign is that of disconnected handwriting. The maximum degree of intensity applies when all letters are disconnected. This sign indicates a tendency towards detailed analysis of the facts and over-attention to detail. In everyday language, these individuals are fussy. In a treatise on graphology from the beginning of the century, they were defined as being 'incapable of love'. This is not altogether true; however, disconnected handwriting does signal an inability to grasp a problem in its entirety and a difficulty in drawing conclusions. Slaves to their habits, these writers tend to remain insolated because of their difficulty in adapting to the every day reality around them. They need to be encouraged to interact more with society both at work and in their leisure time.

*Pythagoras, shown in a detail of a Raphael fresco in the Vatican*

*Disconnected handwriting suggests a fussy, finicky nature*

The balance is restored where both connected and disconnected signs are found, with a slight predominance of the former, when the handwriting shows occasional interruptions between groups of connected letters.

*Portrait of the nineteenth century composer, Giuseppe Verdi*

## Giuseppe Verdi

The son of modest shopkeepers, Giuseppe Verdi was born at Roncole di Busseto in Italy in 1813. Despite a hard-working musical apprenticeship, he was unable to gain entry to the Milan Conservatory and instead went to study under Vincenzo Lavigna, a composer of the Neapolitan school living in Milan. Verdi's first extraordinary success was *Nabucco*, in 1842.

With works such as *Il Trovatore, La Traviata, La Forza del Destino, Falstaff*, and *Don Carlos*, Verdi soon showed himself to be one of the greatest musical talents ever. A complete master of the medium in which he expressed himself, a romantic and very acute man, Verdi had a signature which was distinctive and refined, with a flourish of double underlining. It shows him to have been a scrupulous, rigorous perfectionist.

## Giacomo Puccini

Giacomo Puccini was born in Lucca, Italy, in 1858. He came from a family of musicians who sent him first to the Musical Institute in Lucca and then to the Milan Conservatory.

With its richness of melodic inspiration, originality of harmony and dramatic intensity, *Manon Lescaut* was the opera which first brought success to the Tuscan composer, in 1893. This was followed by *La Bohème* and *Madame Butterfly*. Puccini's work is characterized by its all-consuming poetic atmosphere and great sense of drama. Puccini's signature shows him to have been a precise man, even in the hurried way the lines are drawn: it reveals a feeling for the aesthetic and for everything which is ordered and organized. His own marriage, however, was stormy and unhappy.

Great attention to detail is also revealed by the sporadic signs of disconnected writing in these signatures.

# Constancy in love

*Linked handwriting, when some words are joined, reveals a loyal lover*

## Linking

When the words in handwriting have horizontal extensions connecting them with the beginning of the following word, this characteristic is referred to as the graphological sign of linking.

This handwriting is clearly a more exaggerated version of connected handwriting (see page 56) and therefore expresses the typical tendencies of this sign, accentuating its intensity. Graphological linking also denotes its own particular characteristics.

To fully understand the meaning of the graphic gesture that connects or disconnects letters and words, you need to consider the value assigned to linking both the various elements of the words and the various elements of phrases.

The tendency to connect these elements is in strict relation to the writer's inner logic. A particularly disconnected script denotes a tendency towards detailed analysis, a lack of cohesive activity and an inclination towards fussiness. Connected handwriting, on the other hand, denotes continuity of action and thought and an ability to analyse reality in the broad view. The ideal applies when the two signs are both to be found in the same handwriting. All of this relates primarily to the linking between the letters within a word, but the value of this sign in connections between the various words is also significant.

The mental activity expressed by individuals who join one word to the next is nervous energy and a desire to pass from one element to the next without stopping for critical analysis. People who exhibit the sign of linking in their handwriting also have a remarkable capacity for logic. However, while a logical attitude to problems is positive, it is also true that these individuals lack critical powers to judge elements which may be crucial to the success or failure of a project.

Persons with the sign of linking will persist in seeing through whatever they have undertaken to do, even if it would be more sensible to give up. They always have a clear picture of their objectives and remain faithful to their plans and to their loved ones. Nothing would induce them to betray anyone whom they have chosen as the object of their love, nor would they allow themselves to indulge in an unforeseen love affair that did not fit in with their plans. They will not fall in love at first sight, but only after having given the matter due thought. However, once they have made their decision they will remain in love with that person for ever.

Writers with the linked sign will always tend to follow the thread of their logic, thereby running the risk of not giving due importance to the opinions held by others. They will often appear to be detached from everything that is taking place around them. As a result of this they are not always liked by those who require a certain amount of adaptability and mental flexibility in others.

Overall, this sign denotes little reflection between one phase of thought and the next, a trait which is generally not positive. To give a better balance, the linked sign should be accompanied by other signs indicating critical and reflective powers as otherwise the writer will always be tensed and ready for action, incapable of pausing and weighing up the facts. Overall the sign of linking (which is not common) must be counteracted by other signs in order to express positive values; otherwise it denotes rather tiresome traits.

# Love and marriage

In order for a person's handwriting to reflect his or her character and mental attitudes properly, the sample should be written on unlined paper. This is not only to establish whether it is rising or falling, but also whether it is even or uneven.

## Uneven handwriting

The characteristic feature of graphologically uneven handwriting is an upward or downward slope away from the base line, with sudden movements deviating from the central axis.

Unevenness basically indicates a passionate temperament where instinctive impulses predominate over reason. Those with this sign to a substantial degree will be inclined to be nervous, will allow themselves to be carried away by their impetuosity, and will find it difficult to stop and reflect before they act.

A sense of proportion, awareness of danger and cautiousness are not their distinguishing features: they will always act first without thinking of the risks that they are running. When they make a mistake they realize their limitations, but in spite of their good intentions they will continue to fail to control their impulsiveness.

The most frequent winners in Chicago's College All-Star Game is Green Bay Packers. They compiled a 6-2 record in the

*Uneven handwriting points to a passionate temperament*

They will suffer from inner conflict and will readily swing between calm and anger, friendliness and argumentativeness, without considering the effects of these changes on their minds. They will be sincere to the end in expressing their ideas.

In the field of intellect, this sign denotes liveliness in thought and ideas and, based on the irregularity of the sign, originality and inspiration. These considerations apply only if the sign is present to a conspicuous extent, as otherwise the characteristics stated only exist in marginal form and do not represent important elements of the personality.

## Even handwriting

The opposite sign is evenness, which applies when the letters of the handwriting (particularly the ovals) appear to have been placed in such a way as to rest on the line: the lower part of the letters is squared and flattened, as if it is intended to serve as a support.

Once again the sign is interpreted according to its percentage incidence and in the context of the handwriting as a whole. A high percentage is indicative of seriousness in terms of ideas and intentions, and of resoluteness and courage.

pleasure, and the first crops are almost ready, but keep a look out for the first surge of garden pests.

*If all the letters rest on the base line the handwriting is even*

People whose handwriting shows the sign of evenness exhibit a desire to have a clear mind and to be aware of their own actions at all times. The strong will and steadiness that are characteristic of this sign enable those who write like this to undertake anything that they are certain of being able to see through to the end. They have their feet firmly on the ground and will abide by their commitments and be loyal in their affections. Those who firmly plant their writing on the line are unlikely to be idealists or to be carried away by irrational emotions and impulses.

A further characteristic that emerges from the sign of evenness is caution in action and words, with respect to innovation. The individuals in question do not like sudden changes and will only leave what they are familiar with after due reflection and with appropriate caution.

Remember as always that this sign only becomes significant in the context of the overall evaluation of the writer's script, and that attention must be paid to the presence of confirmatory or contradictory signs. (Harmoniously uneven handwriting will have a very different meaning from that given here.) Only in this way can you be certain of producing a reliable analysis of the handwriting in question.

# A happy marriage

### The signature

The signature of a married woman who uses her husband's surname can reveal much about the success of her marriage. From a graphological viewpoint, the signature comprises two essential elements: the surname and the forename, and in some cases an initial. Handwriting is liable to change in line with the development of the individual's personality over time and sometimes with the mood at the time of writing; a signature, on the other hand, must follow a certain pattern to prove its authenticity.

In the case of families whose members have occupied positions of considerable social and political importance, descendants may copy the signatures of their predecessors in honour of the prestige that they represented in their time. The signature cannot be expected to give a complex view of the individuals' personalities, but it does provide a number of important clues to help identify the events in the past that have affected the way in which the individuals' personalities have developed. The style of the surname can reveal the value that persons have assigned in their life to their family.

The signature is recognized as having an official value and a private value. In the former case writers, particularly if they occupy a public position, are presenting themselves to others. In the latter, it gives their more intimate image of themselves.

*The clearly written surname of a happily married woman*

Children, in the first years of their life, are accustomed to being called solely by their forename, and it is with this name that they identify themselves. It is only when they start school and therefore become social entities that they learn to use their surnames. As children grow up, they attribute a purely social identity value to their signature and may eliminate their forename altogether.

Women tend to attribute greater importance to their forenames, both because for many centuries they live their social role to a lesser extent than men, and because when they are married they abandon their own surname. They tend to retain their forename as bearing witness to their premarital selves, and the larger they write it the greater the importance they attach to their past.

Women who value their married status and who wish to share their husband's social role write their surname clearly; those, on the other hand, who regard the role that they are forced to occupy as a burden tend to write their forename large and, if they dislike their married name, may even omit it. In introductions, men will generally state their surnames (a desire to be recognized socially rather than individually), while women will more readily introduce themselves by their forenames (a desire to demonstrate their individuality). As women begin to occupy more public positions, they are found to give preference to their surname – frequently their maiden name.

The writing of the forename, then, expresses a wide range of meanings. The elements that you need to consider for the purposes of interpretation are: whether it is stated in full or in abbreviated form; the clarity and size of the characters and, finally, the relationship between it and the surname. Where a person gives greater prominence and clarity to his or her forename, this suggests a desire to assign more importance to his or her intimate personality than to his or her official self which is governed by social considerations and ancestral relationships.

Where the signature shows a marked difference between the slope of the forename and that of the surname, this could signify rejection of the individual's family of origin.

Where the forename (abbreviated or otherwise) and the surname are written with a single stroke of the pen, they form an indivisible entity: this shows a desire on the part of the writer to give distinction to his or her forename, either because it is very common, or because it is the same as that of other members of his or her family. Alternatively, it may mean that the writer attributes the same importance to his or her private personality as to his or her public persona.

## Salvador Dali

Salvador Dali was born at Figueras in Catalonia, Spain, in 1904. Dali joined the Surrealist movement in Paris in 1929. His bizarre canvases went far beyond accepted bounds and verged on abstraction, but were created using great technical ability. Dali's signature is dominated by the 'D' of his surname and its ornateness reflects his imagination. Despite his outrageous image, Dali allowed no intrusions into his private life. This flamboyant signature excludes his forename, symbolically protecting his personal concerns.

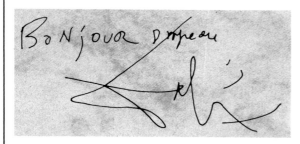

Self Portrait in Front of an Easel *by Vincent Van Gogh*

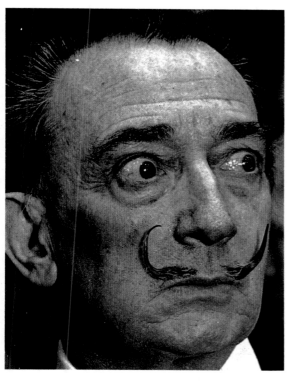

## Vincent Van Gogh

Vincent Van Gogh was born in Groot-Zundert, in Brabant, Holland, in 1853. The son of a Protestant pastor, his acquaintance with art began when he worked in a shop in The Hague, and then later in London and Paris. In 1876 he underwent a religious conversion and was persuaded to become a lay preacher, but when this did not work out he turned to painting. From 1886 his contacts with the French capital brought him closer to the Impressionist movement and the sombre tones of his early paintings were abandoned. Later, during a stay in Arles in 1888, he chose to use colours symbolically. His signature is bleak and harsh, but its strong vertical tendencies show an impassioned nature. By omitting his surname Van Gogh reveals his life-long search for inner meaning and rejection of his family background.

# Love at first sight

Horizontal lines are connected with the field of intelligence, whereas stems relate to willpower. In general, pressure is evident in downward strokes. If it is found in horizontal lines, excessive pressure denotes a predilection to dominate and it implies that the writer wishes to convert other people to his or her own ideas. If it is found in vertical lines it indicates a tendency on the part of the writer to be dictatorial. The intensity of this sign is evaluated by the frequency with which it occurs in the handwriting and in relation to thickness in the ovals and in links between one letter and the next, both at the base and at the top.

## Thick horizontal lines

Thick horizontal lines are produced with the same passion as that with which the writer holds and imposes his or her views. A person with this sign will tend to see reality according to his or her own wishes; he or she lacks serenity of thought and shows a marked aversion to other people's ideas, particularly if they are contrary to his or her own. In taking decisions this person puts passion before reason.

Such people find it difficult to enter into discussions and to change their mind. Emotionally, they are passionate to excess, and in the education of their children they tend to pursue their convictions without considering other people's needs to such an extent that they traumatize those who live around them. They are also lacking in balance in view of the hostility with which they react to external stimuli. They are even prepared to perpetrate psychological violence on others to induce them to share their own views. They are usually tense, unable to relax and do not enjoy the pleasures of life.

## Retracing

Handwriting is described as retraced when some of the letters are redrawn or amended. This phenomenon reveals the writers' need to go back over their past, seeking perfection and clarity. To establish the intensity of this sign, the frequency of blurred or double-edged letters and the corrections made to them has to be calculated.

This sign denotes a marked tendency towards self-correction and writers who show it, while self-confident, nonetheless feel it necessary to go back very carefully over what they have done to improve and check it. They are always ready to change decisions that they have made, and feel a need to verify what they have done because of an excessive sense of responsibility for their actions.

They have strong inhibitions and will give in readily in an argument: they succeed in overcoming crises with those around them through their ability to change their views and their pronounced sense of responsibility.

## Obliteration

The obliterating graphological sign applies when certain letters are constantly misformed to such an extent that they look like other letters. This phenomenon cannot, of course, be extended to all letters, otherwise the alphabet produced would no longer conform to the model.

Obliteration may be caused by excessive nervous energy, or simply by the low level of importance that the writer assigns to accuracy. Care needs to be taken to avoid confusing obliterating handwriting with obscure handwriting. In the former there is systematic confusion between one letter and another, while in the latter the lack of clarity can affect any letter, albeit sporadically.

Individuals who show the graphological sign of obliteration tend towards constant imprecision and are subject to neurotic haste. They learn by approximation and will readily fall into errors and confusion. They show a lack of good sense in their decisions and choices.

Such writers are extremely quick-tempered and impatient and are unable to check their emotional outbursts which are often directed at those around them. They will fall in love on a sudden impulse that they are unable to control as their emotions, passions and rationale are not in proper harmony.

*Tension and charisma are revealed by a distorted, obliterated script*

Under the effects of anger or emotional tension they will show a lack of responsibility and awareness. They prefer a lively atmosphere in which they can give expression to their reactions. They will pursue their activities frenetically and impatiently, and lack any strategy in planning their work; if they perform a management function, they will be unable to give their staff proper instructions and will frequently attack them as a result of their hot temper. They have a substantial amount of aggression which they are unable to channel profitably, instead wasting it on violent and uncontrolled outbursts.

Victory Oct: 19: 1805
Noon Cady ENE 16 Leagues

My Dearest beloved Emma the dear
friend of my bosom the signal has
been made that the Enemys combined
fleet are coming out of Port, We
have very little Wind so that I have
no hopes of seeing them before tomorrow
may the God of Battles crown my
Endeavours with success at all events
I will take care that my name shall ever
be most dear to you and Horatia both
of whom I love as much as my own
life, and as my last writing before the
battle will be to you so I hope in God that
I shall live to finish my letter after the

*Lord Nelson's last letter to his mistress, Lady Hamilton, written just before the Battle of Trafalgar, 1805*

# 5

# Summary

Now you have mastered the basic elements of graphology you will want to embark on analysing some samples of your own. This chapter contains a quick reference list of all the signs that have been covered to make it easier for you in your first experiments. As times goes by, of course, you will memorize more and more of the signs and you will no longer need to look them up. Do remember, as always, that no sign should be considered in isolation as there may be other signs modifying, reinforcing or negating it – and that the qualities given here represent the full percentage of the sign. Combining all the elements together to reach an overall picture is tricky at first, but it will come with practice.

Remember, too, the rules for obtaining handwriting samples: take several written at different times; they should preferably not be written specifically for analysis, as self-consciousness (and the desire to impress) will radically alter someone's writing; and only use samples written in ink on white, unlined paper with no margins, so you can calculate the signs of pressure and rising, straight and falling accurately. When examining your own handwriting, use old scraps you have written. It should not be difficult to find subjects, however. Most people cannot resist a chance to hear about themselves!

*A document written in Sanskrit, the ancient and sacred language of Hindu India*

# Summary

*A detail of the fourteenth century* Tractatus de Sphera *by Joannis de Sacrobosco, Central Library, Bologna*

This chapter contains a list of the signs discussed so far with their most representative character traits, providing you with an easy reference.

## Rising

*Sloping upwards from the baseline.*

Uncontrolled energy with generosity and expansiveness: optimism, with superficiality and vanity: arrogance, with a good intellect and sound will: the ability to better oneself.

## Straight
*Keeping to the baseline.*

Strength of will, balance and self-control.

## Falling
*Descending below the baseline.*

Weak will and lack of moral fibre; easily influenced character, mental fragility, depression, unease, lack of confidence; rapid shifting from melancholy to depression.

## Right hand slant
*Letter slanting to the right.*

Ability to absorb other people's ideas and experiences. With narrow letters: originality; to excess: tendency towards discouragement; melancholy; need for gratification; expansiveness, persuasive powers, charming manners.

## Left hand slant
*Letters slanting to the left.*

Intellect and willpower; irritability, hostility, sullenness.

## Forced
*Constant distortion in formation.*

Aversion for the outside world; mental constraint; inability to abstract information; narrow mindedness, indecision; limited imagination, little creativity; tension, stress, exhaustion.

## Distorted
*Deformation of certain letters in relation to the copybook style.*

Desire to be different; difficulty in concentrating and assimilating facts; rigidity in the affections; pessimism, sadness.

## Broad letters
*Widely formed letters.*

Great intelligence, realism, rationality, aptitude for scientific research; introspection, discretion, depth.

There are two people who particularly come to mind when discussing childish handwriting. Both were infant prodigies: Wolfgang Amadeus Mozart and Shirley Temple.

Each had very different temperaments and careers, but as children they owed part of their fame to the fact that both were performing what are normally adult roles at an unusually early age. The signatures of both reflect their early maturity.

*A portrait of Mozart playing the piano, aged eleven*

## Mozart

Mozart was only six when Maria Teresa of Austria summoned him to the Court at Vienna. By the age of fourteen he was able to write a concerto in the space of one hour and had become a phenomenon talked about by the whole of Europe. His heavily underscored signature shows decisiveness and firmness, together with a certain amount of arrogance.

## Shirley Temple

Shirley Temple was the idol of America in the thirties. Every little girl wanted to look like this pretty, golden haired creature who appeared beside many of the greatest actors and actresses of the age. But by the time she reached the age of twelve her fortunes were on the wane, and the three hundred thousand dollars a year she had earned at the peak of her career was becoming a memory. Her handwriting reveals the almost unnaturally early maturity of a child adored by the crowds who watched her.

Both children's handwriting leans to the right, suggesting charm and a need for attention from others.

## Narrow letters
*Narrow letters.*

With sharpness and spikiness: sharp intelligence but with little depth of thought; superficial haste; loss of the central core of problems; irony, sarcasm and general irritability towards others.

## Curl of concealment
*Endstroke turned back underneath the last letter.*

Concealment of true self, reserve, reticence; caution, mistrust; self-control, formal courtesy, diplomacy; precision, insincerity.

## Wide apart
*Difference in direction of stems and loops.*

Memory that is able to discern concepts and ideas acquired over a long period of time; clarity of thought and concepts; lawfulness, order, cleanliness; also a tendency to be mean.

## Muddled
*Confusion between stems and loops.*

Confusion, chaos, vagueness; tendency towards misunderstanding; gaps in the memory; excessive talkativeness; lack of consistency; lack of self-criticism; anger; irrationality.

## Conceited movement
*Capital letters drawn to excess.*

Pomposity, extremely high opinion of self; coarseness, pushiness, excessive self-assurance; little self-criticism; irascibility, narcissism, dishonesty; arrogance, authoritarianism, egocentricity.

## Backward movement
*Capital letters drawn to excess with backward turn to left.*

Morbid attachment to memories; failure to make positive moves in the present or for the future; readiness to mourn.

## Upright stems
*Perpendicular to the baseline.*

Inflexibility of character; independence in ideas and affections; defence of inner self; aggression, if combined with signs of enterprise; incorruptibility.

## Stems curving forwards
*Concave part to the right.*

Submits in judgement and behaviour; flexibility.

## Stems curving backwards
*Concave part to the left.*

Rejection of new ideas; defence of inner self; sharpness and narrowness between letters adds to the defects.

## Long 't' crosses
*More than one oval plus a space.*

Aggression, passion, impetuosity; prone to command, irritability, anger.

## Short 't' crosses
*Less than one oval's width.*

Fixed ideas, memory blocks, indecision; lacks passion.

## Thick 't' crosses
*Thick cross over the stem of the 't'.*

Tendency to command, domineering personality, distortion of reality; lack of self-criticism.

## Thin 't' crosses
*Thin cross over the stem of the 't'.*

Delicacy of expression, weak will, timidity.

## Thickening 't' crosses
*Crosses becoming thicker as they proceed to the right.*

Tendency to command; irritability.

*A painting depicting St Matthew, from Louis XIV's art collection at Versailles*

### Boris Karloff

Boris Karloff, or Charles Edward Pratt, was born in Dulwich in 1887. In 1919 he made the great leap into the world of cinema. He became famous throughout the world for playing the monster Frankenstein, and for the rest of his career he specialized in horror roles. His autograph has a fairly high dot over the 'i', indicating that he had difficulties with his feelings.

### William Powell

Born in Pittsburgh in 1892, William Powell was one of the best actors in the history of the American cinema. He made his first appearance on the New York stage in 1912, and on the silver screen ten years later. With his impeccable, naturally rhythmic voice, he became a sensational success with the arrival of sound. Elegant and careful in his manners and dress, he was an extremely likeable character with a shrewd expression.

Powell played two of the most successful cinema detectives, Philo Vance and the brilliant Nick Charles. At his side was Myrna Loy, with her inimitable charm.

It is impossible to find a single bad film which Powell was involved with over the many years of his long career. He died in 1984, and his signature, which has comparatively low dots over the 'i's', demonstrates a great pleasure in both the material and the hedonistic aspects of life.

**Thinning 't' crosses**
*Crosses becoming thinner as they proceed to the right.*

Hypersensitivity.

**Incorporated 't' crosses**
*'T' cross incorporated in the stem.*

Practicality, ingenuity, impatience, hastiness.

**Repeated 't' crosses**
*'T' crossed twice.*

Seeks clarity; self-criticism, emotional, prone to guilt.

**Balanced upper and lower extensions**
*Upper and lower extensions of equal length.*

Self harmony, control over wastefulness and greed.

**Excessive lower extensions**
*Lower extensions much longer than upper extensions.*

Need for recognition; wasted energy; love of luxury.

**Excessive upper extensions**
*Upper extensions much longer than lower extensions.*

Self detriment due to idealism and rationality; escapism.

**Excessive upper and lower extensions**

Contrasting impulses; lack of balance.

**High 'i' dots**
*Dot more than halfway up the upper extension.*

Unrealistic, incapable of understanding others.

**'I' dots omitted**

Carelessness, negligence, poor memory.

**Low 'i' dots**
*Very close to the stem of the 'i'.*

Assignment of excessive importance to material details; quibbling nature; meanness in sharing material goods.

**Central 'i' dots**
*Dot immediately above the stem of the 'i'.*

Quibbling nature, precision, attention to unimportant details; little practicality; wastage of energy, inhibitions, control of the emotions with sudden outbursts.

**'I' dots to the right**
*Dots to the right of the stem of the 'i'.*

Affectation, artificiality, nervous energy; ability to absorb concepts.

**Connected 'i' dots**
*Dots written without lifting the pen from the paper.*

Powers of logic and synthesis; practicality; consistency of thought.

**Dash-like 'i' dots**
*Extended 'i' dot.*

Anxiety; need for precision and accuracy; sense of responsibility.

**Circle dots**
*Roundly formed 'i' dots.*

Stubbornness, aggression, fussiness, quibbling nature, immaturity.

**Systematic inequality**
*Harmonious inequality in size of letters.*

Originality, creativity, imagination; perspicacity, intelligence, flair, intuition; artistic sense, richness of ideas and thought; desire for innovation; emotional intensity and immediacy.

**Disorderliness**
*Lack of proportion between the elements of the handwriting.*

Disorderliness in ideas and intentions; vagueness of thought and feelings; lack of coherence, objectivity and consistency; distraction, fickleness, disquiet, turbulence; impulsiveness, aimlessness, recklessness; little reflectiveness; excessive enthusiasm.

**Obscure**
*Obscure, illegible letters.*

Obscurity and indeterminacy in ideas, actions and thoughts; difficulties in expression, vagueness, ambiguity; tendency towards isolation; difficulty in human relations, loss of self confidence.

**Speed**
*Hasty handwriting with no stops.*

Quickness in behaviour, disregard of details, swift conclusions; spontaneity, readiness of expression; energy, diligence, speed in gestures and actions.

**Slowness**
*Lazy, phlegmatic style.*

Immobility; slowness in grasping concepts, processing information and taking action; laziness. To excess: lack of willpower, sang-froid, fatigue, listlessness.

**Calm**
*No surges, pressure or curls.*

Self-assurance, stability, regularity; thoughtfulness, caution, balance; serenity, self-control, impassivity; fairness in judgements, punctuality, courtesy, respectability.

**Meticulousness**
*Handwriting almost printed.*

Precise, methodical; stereotyped language; absence of passion and imagination; attached to habits, conformist, punctual; narrow minded.

**Equality**
*Precision in size.*

A variant of meticulousness: mechanical reproduction of form; uniformity, traditionalism; absence of personal refashioning of ideas.

**Pedantry**
*Presence of aesthetic touches and contrast.*

Like equality, this is a variant of meticulousness. The equality traits apply, plus a closed mind and no warmth.

**Clear**
*Clear and legible letters.*

Discernment, precision; courtesy, order, polish; spontaneity, affectionate; reliability, respectability.

**Impatience**
*Indistinct, blurred or omitted letters.*

Little self-control; irascibility, excitability; impatience, hastiness, superficiality; nervous energy, chaotic nature, convulsive gestures, impulsiveness.

**Dynamic**
*Spirally linked letters.*

Incessant activity in thought and action; meanness; clarity of expression; simplicity, incisiveness, sincerity; enthusiasm for action, loyalty.

**Wavering**
*Letters leaning in different directions.*

Indecisiveness, instability; difficulty in completing things; insecurity, dependence, awkwardness.

**Polished**
*Precise style and small size.*

Courtesy, clarity of thought, gentleness, characteristics accompanied by affectation; adaptability; lack of scruples; attention to detail, refinement.

*Portrait of François I, a witty and cultured French king.*

## François I

François I, King of France, was born in Cognac in 1494. He came to the throne in 1515 following the death, without any heir, of his cousin Louis XII. At the time France was experiencing a period of economic and commercial prosperity. Fickle, ambitious, cultured and quick-witted, François I established a magnificent court around himself, laying the foundations of the splendour of the French monarchy. He was a dedicated patron of literature and the arts, and in foreign policy he distinguished himself by his inclination for war. His autograph shows meticulousness: it is written in an extremely elegant style and he has taken obsessive care with the individual letters, which look almost as if they were printed.

## Catherine the Great

The great Empress of Russia, Catherine II, was born in Stettin on 2 May 1729. She married the Grand Duke Peter, who later became Emperor and was known as Peter III. When her powerful husband died following a plot in which Catherine was involved, she herself inherited the imperial throne. Although of German nationality, Catherine was fierce in the defence of Russia. Her enlightened despotism enabled her to introduce some major reforms, although she was hampered in these by the private interests of the Russian nobility. The Empress nonetheless made a place for herself in history by reconstructing the administrative and judicial system and promoting art and literature. Her signature is an example of clear handwriting. It is relatively simple with a long bar across the entire word – the sign of a resolute character.

*Catherine II, the clever, magnanimous Empress of Russia*

## Precise
*Studied style.*

Lack of spontaneity, precision in speech, written language, dress etc; meticulousness, self-control, rigidity; insincerity, lack of imagination.

## Solemn
*Pompous style with pressure on downstrokes.*

Self-importance; meticulous attention to the person, respect for dignity; rigid and authoritarian in the affections.

## Arrogant
*Large, showy letters.*

Megalomania, rudeness, pushiness, excessive self-confidence out of proportion with the individual's true abilities and skills; excessive optimism, ostentatiousness, lack of balance and sense of proportion; distortion of reality.

## Plain
*No curls, small size.*

Sobriety, brevity, down-to-earth thought, ideas, actions, language; moderation, coherence, composure, fairness, strong morality.

## Self-moderation
*Flowing, without omitting 'i' dots and with 'a', 'g', 'p', 'r', 's' and 'z' in accordance with the copybook style.*

Self-discipline, clarity of expression and ideas; lucidity, mental vigour, loyalty; control of the passions and emotions; equilibrium, wilfulness, efficient and well organized.

## Wide spacing between letters
*Spacing between one letter and the next.*

Consideration of others; safeguarding of inner self; attentiveness; objectivity, generosity, open-mindedness; excessive optimism; recklessness, fool-hardiness, naivety.

## Narrow spacing between letters
*Little space between one letter and the next.*

Closed mind and withdrawal into self; jealousy, envy, meanness.

## Profusion
*Excessive spacing between letters.*

Intellectual and physical waste; consumerism; excessive generosity; excessive altruism to the detriment of self.

## Tightly packed
*Letters tightly packed together.*

Timidity in the intellect and affections; fear of making a mistake; pessimism, discouragement, physical delicacy.

## Wide spacing between words
*Large space between words.*

Global view of reality; balance, rationality, logic; maturity in processing, understanding and abstracting facts; aptitude for scientific research; hypercritical; argumentativeness, rigidity.

## Narrow spacing between words
*Little space between one word and the next.*

Poor powers of criticism and thought; superficiality.

## Connected
*Connected letters, or few breaks.*

Continuity of thought and action; powers of logic and deduction; ability to summarize; coherence, consistency; lack of reflection and attention.

## Disconnected
*Disconnected letters.*

Analytical powers; observation of details; difficulties in summarizing; attachment to habit.

*A portrait of Diego Martelli by the nineteenth century Italian painter, Federico Zandomeneghi*

*A lady sealing a letter by Jean Baptiste Simeon Chardin, the eighteenth century French painter*

### Linked
*Letters and words connected.*

Powers of logic; poor critical powers; loyalty; absence of powers of reflection; closed mind.

### Uneven
*Letters not keeping to the baseline.*

Nervous energy, impetuosity, imprudence; inner conflict, impulsiveness, hot temper; originality, flair, unshakable idealism.

### Even
*Letters firmly planted on the baseline.*

Thoughtfulness, seriousness, resoluteness; courage, self-control, solidity, caution.

### Thick horizontal lines
*Thickening of horizontal strokes.*

Predominance of passion over reason, causing psychological violence to others; tension.

### Retraced
*Letters that are retraced or amended.*

Excessive self-correction; the need to revise what has already been done; excessive sense of responsibility; ability to change one's mind.

### Obliterating
*Letters constantly distorted.*

Excessive dynamism; little precision; irritability; imbalance between emotions, passions and rationality.

*A portrait of an unknown man writing, by Giovanni Carnovali, otherwise known as 'Il Piccio'*

# 6

# Dictionary of Graphology

The way in which an individual letter can be written has infinite variations – and each has a tale to tell. It is one of the most fascinating features of handwriting that although most people start, as children, copying from the same model, in no time at all their personality impresses itself on their writing and the copybook letters flower into sometimes quite disparate versions of the original. The style in which each letter is written has its own significance, even down to such tiny details as to whether an endstroke finishes just above or just below the baseline. Some of the meanings are almost self-evident; a narrow, hunched capital letter perfectly mirrors the demeanour of a shy and timid person when faced with a situation which makes him uneasy. Sometimes they are less obvious – a person presenting you with a capital 'B' hooked to the left is not likely to have any idea that his or her writing has just told you he or she is avaricious!

It is not feasible to include all the many possible variations here – different Nations have different styles and, as well, there will always be those who have originated a letter formed in a fashion peculiar to themselves. However, the following list encompasses all of the more common variations you are likely to encounter, as well as some of the more unusual ones.

*Sixteenth century woodblocks, used to illustrate the legend of the Arthurian hero Perceval*

# A

| | | | | | | |
|---|---|---|---|---|---|---|
| A | Low crossbar | Discipline, precision | | a | Printed letter | Artistic temperament |
| A | High crossbar | Superiority | | a | Open at bottom | Reserved nature, hypocrisy |
| A | Tall and narrow | Shyness, inhibition | | a | Knotted on left | Animosity, anxiety |
| A | Crossed at top | Initiative, non-conformity | | a | Ink-filled | Sensuality |
| A | Crossbar omitted | Carelessness | | a | Square (lower case) | Manual dexterity |
| A | Descending crossbar | Melancholy, disappointment | | a | Balanced, knotted | Enterprising spirit, shrewdness |
| A | Hooked on left | Shrewdness, calculating nature | | a | Descending | Shyness |
| A | Hooked on right | Egotism | | a | Well-defined starting stroke | Caution |
| a | Written same as small letter | Modesty, reserved nature | | a | Partially closed | Sexual fantasies |
| a | Same as small letter, open | Happiness, simplicity | | a | Endstroke rising | Excitability, enthusiasm |
| A | Continuous line | Arrogance, self-assurance | | a | Endstroke descending | Melancholy |
| A | Balanced, extended crossbar | Balanced personality | | a | Wavy endstroke | Firmness |
| a | Looped and open | Efficiency, self-assurance | | d | Sharp angle | Ambition |
| A | Open at top | Talkativeness, cordiality | | a | Broad and closed | Aptitude for science |
| A | Square | Manual dexterity | | a | Broad and open | Sincerity |
| A | Wavy crossbar | Imagination | | u | Double ink-filled knots | Delusion, animosity |
| A | Crossbar rising | Communicativeness | | e | Unbalanced, knotted | Tendency to fantasize, delicacy |
| A | Circular crossbar | Affectation, exhibitionism | | e | Narrow and knotted | Sensitivity |
| A | Vertical crossbar | Introversion | | a | Protected | Introversion |

# B

| | | |
|---|---|---|
| B | Wide lower section | Naivety |
| B | Sloping, with in-flated upper section | Arrogance |
| B | Narrow letter | Shyness, inhibition |
| B | Hook to left | Avarice |
| B | Like figure 13 | Good memory |
| B | Very angular | Hardness, cruelty |
| B | Inflated lower section | Self-important |
| B | Tall vertical stroke | Enterprise |
| B | Large opening at baseline | Introspection |
| B | Small opening at baseline | Talkativeness, sociability |
| B | Starting endstrokes extended to left | Determination, precision |
| b | Very open | Naivety |
| b | Looped endstroke | Imagination |
| b | Full upper loop | Fantasy, expressiveness |
| b | Without upper loop | Taste, intelligence |
| b | Starting stroke below baseline | Resentment, argumentativeness |
| b | Tightly closed | Caution, business ability |
| b | Small circle on starting stroke | Jealousy towards a particular person |
| b | Ink-filled upper loop | Sensuality |

# C

| | | |
|---|---|---|
| C | Square | Mechanical and constructive skill |
| C | Starting with a hook | Enjoyment of material success |
| C | Scrolled at bottom | Egotism |
| C | Loop at top | Vanity |
| C | Narrow | Shyness, reserve |
| C | Scrolled at top | Shrewdness, opportunism |
| C | Rounded and full | Idealism, naivety |
| C | Ornate | Vulgar taste |
| C | Angle at base | Tendency to bear grudges, obstinacy |
| c | Pointed at top | Penetrating intellect |
| c | Rounded | Gentleness |
| c | Almost closed | Pronounced reserve |
| c | Starting with closed loop | Business ability |
| c | Simple | Simple, straightforward |
| c | Angular | Quick mind |
| e | Large, with straight starting stroke | Kindliness, optimism |
| c | Angle at base | Insistence, resentment |
| e | Starting stroke through letter | Calculating mind |
| e | Like letter 'e' | Egotism |

# D

| | | |
|---|---|---|
| | Closed, with a large loop | Caution |
| | Very wide | Love of luxury |
| | Very broad but not square | Vanity |
| | With a starting stroke | Impatience, irritability |
| | Very angular | Hardness, malice |
| | Unusual shape | Imagination and eroticism |
| | Looped, with rising endstroke | Prospect of love |
| | Diagonal rising endstroke | Ambition |
| | Extended starting and endstrokes | Good powers of concentration |
| | Long starting stroke below baseline | Argumentativeness |
| | Claw on endstroke | Avarice, greed |
| | Wide open at top | Frivolity |
| | Wide open at baseline | Desire for self-knowledge |
| | Two separate strokes | Individualism |
| | Hook on starting stroke | Lack of self-assurance |
| | Tall first stroke | Initiative |
| | Heart-shaped | Romantic nature |
| | Endstroke extended to left | Self-important |
| | Open at top | Sincerity, talkativeness |

| | | |
|---|---|---|
| | Narrow loop | Emotional repression |
| | Open | Talkativeness |
| | Like a musical note | Creativity, artistic interests |
| | Like a Greek letter | Love of culture |
| | Straddled | Love of tranquillity |
| | Endstroke falling below baseline | Obstinacy |
| | Wide loop | Sensitivity, vanity |
| | Knotted | Tendency towards self-deception |
| | Covering stroke on stem | Good listener |
| | Reversed letter 'd' | Rebelliousness |
| | Lasso loop | Interest in poetry |
| | Ink-filled | Sensuality |
| | Closed | Tendency towards secretiveness |
| | Knot on stem | Extreme reserve |
| | Long starting stroke below baseline | Tendency to bear grudges |
| | Tall, wide loop | Love of singing |
| | Short stem | Humility, independence |
| | Open at baseline | Hypocrisy |
| | Hook on starting stroke | Possessiveness |

# E

| | | |
|---|---|---|
| | Extended middle stroke | Caution |
| | Looped starting stroke | Difficulty in managing own affairs |
| | Hook on starting stroke | Greed |
| | Two full arcs | Very quick mind |
| | Long starting stroke below baseline | Tendency to bear grudges |
| | Amended | Insecurity, eccentricity |
| | Ornate | Avarice |
| | Short starting stroke with loop | Sense of style |
| | Narrow | Reserve |
| | Greek form | Cultural refinement |
| | Endstroke curling under to left | Reflectiveness, egotism |
| | Endstroke with downturned hook | Dislike of criticism |
| | High-rising endstroke | A dreamer |
| | Endstroke descending to right | Shyness |
| | No endstroke | Caution, reserved nature |
| | Endstroke rising | Courage |
| | Endstroke turned downwards | Lack of enthusiasm |
| | Endstroke with hook | Tenacity, outspokenness |
| | Endstroke falling below baseline | Hot temper |

# F

| | | |
|---|---|---|
| | Upward hook on left | Dry humour, down-to-earth |
| | Down-pointing top bar | Hardness, rudeness |
| | Wavy top bar | Egotism, exhibitionist |
| | Rising top bar | Desire to prove oneself |
| | Narrow | Reserve |
| | Downward hook on right | Obstinacy, strong will |
| | Extended middle stroke | Caution |
| | Downward hook on left | Reluctance to participate |
| | Tall first stroke | Initiative |
| | Very long top bar | Ambitious |
| | Triangular lower loop | Domestic tyrant |
| | Full upper loop | Open mind, flexibility |
| | Large upper loop, no lower loop | Inventiveness |
| | Cruciform | Mystic leanings |
| | Large lower loop, no upper loop | Sound practical sense |
| | Balanced | Organized mind, business ability |
| | Pointed lower loop | Reluctance to compromise |
| | Knotted | Secretiveness |
| | Very large upper loop | Very emotional nature |

# G

| | Looped starting stroke | Disorganization, absentmindedness |
|---|---|---|
| | Heavy pressure on downstroke | Discontent |
| | Snake-like | Tendency to turn nasty under pressure |
| | Greek form | Culture, refinement |
| | Wide open at top | Inability to keep a secret |
| | Like figure 9 | Concentration |
| | Hook to left | Greed |
| | Straight downstroke | Agile mind |
| | Straight, short downstroke | Ambition, critical mind |
| | Arc to left | Avoidance of responsibility |
| | Very large lower loop | Vivid erotic imagination |
| | Large triangle in lower zone | Domestic tyrant |
| | Endstroke to right | Altruism |
| | Large lower loop | Materialism |
| | Hook on endstroke | Self-love |
| | Hook to left | Avarice |
| | Arc to left | Lack of interest in responsibility |
| | Loop to left | Erotic vanity |
| | Endstroke to right and returning to left | Good intentions not fulfilled |

# H

| | Like a gate | Impatience, impulsiveness |
|---|---|---|
| | Angular, with pressure | A definite character |
| | Downward hook on left | Reluctance to participate |
| | Wavy crossbar | Sense of humour |
| | Convex first downstroke | Firmness of character |
| | Second downstroke taller | Initiative |
| | Downward hook on right | Craving for money and possessions |
| | Like letter N | Frankness |
| | Additional stroke before crossbar | Dislike of interference |
| | Hook on left of bar | Down-to-earth personality |
| | Wavy starting stroke | Sense of humour |
| | Snake-like middle zone | Volubility |
| | Rounded middle zone | Gentleness, simplicity |
| | Very wide loop | Very emotional nature |
| | Angular | Aggression |
| | Long starting stroke | Tendency to bear grudges |
| | Square top to loop | Rigidity, tenacity |
| | Endstroke falling below baseline | Stubbornness |
| | Small loop at top | Day-dreamer |

# I

| | | |
|---|---|---|
| / | Single stroke | Intelligence, spontaneity |
| 2 | Tall, with hook at base | Authoritativeness |
| 7 | Falling below baseline | Cunning, deceit |
| 9 | Over-inflated upper loop | Egocentricity |
| 2 | Loops ending to right | Tendency to find fault with others |
| 3 | Endstroke rising to left | Contemplation |
| 7 | Angular | Tenacity |
| 4 | Like figure 4 | Inability to understand others |
| 9 | Small top loop, curled endstroke | Inferiority complex |
| i | Dot directly above | Precise nature |
| ι | Dot omitted | Absent-mindedness |
| ι | Dot very high | Lack of realism |
| ι | Dot to right | Good powers of observation |
| ι | Dot-like vertical stroke | Firm principles |
| ι | Dot low and directly above | Good powers of concentration |
| ι | Weak dot | Lack of energy |
| ι | Dot low, with heavy pressure | Strong will |
| ι | Dot to left | Caution, prudence |
| ι | Dot-like backward dash | Resentful temperament |

# J

| | | |
|---|---|---|
| J | Like scales | Wavering in ideas |
| 2 | Hook to left | Avarice |
| J | Starting stroke from right | Artistic talent, exhibitionism |
| J | Wavy top bar | Sense of humour |
| J | Exaggerated loop to left | Musicial interests |
| J | Arc to left | Avoidance of responsibility |
| J | Top bar above stem | Cunning |
| J | Large loop in lower zone | Erotic fantasy, love of money |
| J | Large loop in upper zone | Day-dreamer |
| j | Claw to left | Greed |
| j | Endstroke rounded to left | Impressionable |
| j | Dot high to right | Curiosity, impatience |
| i | Straight downstroke | Good judgement |
| j | Endstroke to right | Altruism, liveliness |
| j | Endstroke curved to left | Immaturity |
| j | Very small loop | Lack of vitality |
| j | Dot to left | Caution, prudence |
| j | Large loop | Egotism, narcissism |
| j | Heavy, thick dot | Strong will |

## K

| | | |
|---|---|---|
| | Endstroke descending vertically | Frankness |
| | Separate strokes | Individualism |
| | Endstroke descending below baseline | Defensive instinct |
| | Tall first stroke | Initiative |
| | Like letter R | Eccentricity |
| | Three separate strokes | Organizational talent |
| | Endstroke short of baseline | Ambition |
| | Concave second stroke | Desire to command |
| | Hook top left | Reserve |
| | Tall first stroke | Initiative |
| | Very long starting stroke | Tendency to harbour grudges |
| | Endstroke descending below baseline | Defensive instinct |
| | Over-inflated loop to right | Rebelliousness |
| | Various breaks in loop | Emotional disturbance |
| | Endstroke encircled | Egotism, narcissism |
| | Endstroke descending to left | Reluctance to compromise |
| | Narrow | Inhibition |
| | Downstroke of upper loop very weak | Reluctance to look back over the past |
| | Upstroke of upper loop very faint | Reluctance to face the future |

## L

| | | |
|---|---|---|
| | Hook on starting stroke | Avarice |
| | Small loop at top of stem | Jealousy |
| | Pound sign | Love of money |
| | Like figure 2 | Difficulty in relationships |
| | Starting stroke from right | Exhibitionism |
| | Very narrow | Shyness |
| | Large loop to left | Vanity |
| | Endstroke encircled | Narcissism |
| | Large upper loop | Generosity |
| | Two individual lines | Pragmatism |
| | Curved | Romanticism |
| | Closed loop | Secretiveness |
| | Small loop | Timidity |
| | Over-extended endstroke | Excessive caution |
| | Without loop | Good judgement |
| | Large, full loop | Sensitivity |
| | Long starting stroke from below baseline | Irritability |
| | Very broad loop | Imagination |
| | Square top to loop | Obstinacy |

# M

| | | |
|---|---|---|
| | Broadly spaced | Arrogant |
| | Three loops | Stable person |
| | Angular top and base | Hardness, moral strictness |
| | First hump very tall | Very high opinion of oneself |
| | Middle stroke peaked | Harshness, pride |
| | Inverted | Delicacy |
| | Looped centre | Desire to control others |
| | First stroke starting from right | Volubility |
| | Curled | Little ability to handle obligations |
| | Tall starting stroke | Egotism |
| | Like a crown | Desire to lead |
| | Full circle starting stroke | Sensitivity |
| | Like letter 'u' | Hypochondria |
| | Small circle on starting stroke | Jealousy |
| | Endstroke falling to right | Farsightedness |
| | Decreasing second hump | Diplomacy |
| | Horizontal starting stroke | Severity |
| | High arches | Artistic talent |
| | Thread | Indecision |

# N

| | | |
|---|---|---|
| | Starting with loop | Self-deprecation |
| | Endstroke to left | Fearful nature |
| | Hook on endstroke | Tenacity, strength |
| | Endstroke descending | Lack of sociability |
| | Horizontal starting stroke | Brusque nature, abruptness |
| | Circle on starting stroke | Jealousy, envy |
| | Narrow | Shyness |
| | Tall, hooked starting stroke | Arrogance |
| | Starting stroke lower | Self-consciousness |
| | Endstroke short of baseline | Very reserved |
| | Endstroke with pressure | Brusque manner |
| | Square | Manual dexterity |
| | Angular | Analytical mind |
| | Like letter 'u' | Gentleness, pleasantness |
| | Very broad | Extravagance |
| | Second stroke higher | Naivety |
| | Wavy line | Diplomacy, shrewdness |
| | Hook on starting stroke | Acquisitiveness |
| | Wavy endstroke | Versatility, imagination |

# O

| | | |
|---|---|---|
| | Large knot | Confusion |
| | Teardrop | Arrogance, boastfulness |
| | Like figure 6 | Craving for money |
| | Full and broad | Generosity |
| | Open at baseline | Hypocrisy |
| | Double circle to left | Carelessness |
| | Very narrow | Shyness |
| | Double circle to right | Extreme carelessness |
| | Open at top | Sincerity |
| | High-flying endstroke | Quick mind |
| | Like letter 'e' | Laziness |
| | Double looped within | Lack of self-discipline |
| | Like figure 6 reversed | Imagination |
| | Narrow | Secretiveness |
| | Like a horseshoe | Desire to control others |
| | Open and looped to right | Inability to keep a secret |
| | Open to right | Tendency to speak one's mind openly |
| | Broad and full | Open-mindedness |
| | Crossed at top like letter 'x' | Unreliability |

# P

| | | |
|---|---|---|
| | Quick stroke | Tendency to prevaricate |
| | Angular, with pressure | Aggressive nature |
| | Endstroke to left | Discretion |
| | Square | Manual dexterity |
| | Two separate strokes | Individualism |
| | Very small | Shyness |
| | Very tall | Pride, vanity |
| | Loops on both sides | Self-interest |
| | Loop to left | Dedication to duty |
| | Starting from left in two separate parts | Narcissism |
| | Open at top | Good communicator |
| | Two separate arcs | Manual dexterity |
| | Open on baseline, long lower loop | Rudeness, hardness |
| | Tall starting stroke | Initiative |
| | Peak on starting stroke | Sensitivity, calm outlook |
| | Curled endstroke | Curiosity |
| | Pointed | Goodness of heart |
| | Long lower loop | Love of physical activity |
| | Tall angle in upper zone | Argumentative |

# Q

| | | |
|---|---|---|
| | Narrow | Shyness |
| | Pressure on downward stroke | Vitality, energy |
| | Large knot | Sense of pride |
| | Like figure 2 | Inability to form lasting relationship |
| | Pressure on horizontal stroke | Brusque, abrupt manner |
| | Open at baseline | Hypocrisy, dishonesty |
| | Loop to left | Low self-esteem |
| | Very broad | Open-mindedness |
| | Large loop | Secretiveness |
| | Open at top | Volubility |
| | Arc to left | Superficiality |
| | Knot inside oval | Reserve |
| | Extended endstroke | Self-admiration |
| | Claw to left | Extreme avarice |
| | Triangular lower zone | Dislike of interference |
| | Heavy pressure on downstroke | Strong will |
| | Short lower zone | Physical weakness |
| | Extended top stroke | Need for appreciation |
| | Stem extended to right | Warm-heartedness |

# R

| | | |
|---|---|---|
| | Angular and knotted | Caution, efficiency |
| | Tall and full | Egotism |
| | Square | Manual dexterity |
| | Open at top | Volubility |
| | Inflated upper loop | Kindness, friendliness |
| | Two separate strokes | Decisiveness |
| | Endstroke falling below baseline | Obstinacy, temper |
| | Tall first stroke | Initiative |
| | Centre loop and curled endstroke | Pride, haughtiness |
| | Looped top | A day-dreamer |
| | Large loop on first stroke | Self-importance |
| | Flattened top | Open-mindedness |
| | Simple | Quick mind, shrewdness |
| | Like letter 'v' | Muddler |
| | Extended endstroke | Generosity |
| | Rounded and simple | Dullness, placidity |
| | Pointed top | Sensitivity, honesty |
| | Starting loop | Shyness |
| | Like figure 2 | Mathematical mind |

# S

| | | |
|---|---|---|
| | Arc at baseline | Poor sense of responsibility |
| | Very tall and simple | Imagination |
| | Long starting stroke | Hard-working |
| | Large loop to left | Expansiveness |
| | Looped at baseline | Mental agility |
| | Angular | Aggression |
| | Very narrow | Extreme shyness |
| | Claw on starting stroke | Miserliness |
| | Extended endstroke | Initiative |
| | Snake-like | Shrewdness |
| | Narrow (lower case) | Shyness |
| | Rounded top | Docility |
| | Like a horseshoe | Desire to control others |
| | Tightly closed | Difficulty in communicating |
| | Closed with loop at baseline | Caution |
| | Open at baseline | Expansiveness |
| | Very rounded | Kindness |
| | Open with loop at base | Tenacity |
| | Very sharp top | Critical nature |

# T

| | | |
|---|---|---|
| | Top bar rounded on both sides | Desire for fame |
| | Gracefully ornate | Artistic temperament |
| | Whip-like | Tendency to ill-treat others |
| | Simple | Open mind |
| | Angled with extension to right | Iron will |
| | Like scales | Indecisiveness |
| | Top bar looped to left | Egotism |
| | Top bar separate from stem | High ambitions |
| | Like capital letter 'X' | Depression |
| | High cross to right | Leadership qualities |
| | Cross with upturned hook to right | Tenacity, strength |
| | Middle cross through stem | Caution |
| | Curved cross | Self-indulgence |
| | Cross with down-stroke tick to left | Deep envy |
| | Bowed stem, like letter 'e' | False friendliness |
| | Curled cross | A day-dreamer |
| | Cross away from stem | Enjoyment of challenge |
| | Cross to left of stem | Desire to command |
| | Long cross to right of stem | Sense of responsibility |

# U

| | Wavy line | Diplomacy, tact |
|---|---|---|
| | Very broad | Vivid imagination |
| | Horseshoe | Tendency to prevaricate |
| | Narrow | Shyness, inhibition |
| | Straight starting stroke below baseline | Aggression |
| | Hooked starting stroke | Obstinacy, tenacity |
| | Snake-like | Devious nature |
| | Tall second stroke | Initiative |
| | Straight starting stroke | Attachment to the past |
| | Rounded | Kindliness |
| | Square | Manual dexterity |
| | Deep and broad | Tendency to dramatize |
| | Open at baseline | Hypocrisy |
| | Very angular | Inflexibility |
| | Wavy | Versatility |
| | Looped | Goodness of heart |
| | Long, curved starting stroke | Sense of humour |
| | Droplet | Pessimism |
| | Short second stroke | Absent-mindedness |

# V

| | Like capital letter 'X' | Disloyalty, untruthfulness |
|---|---|---|
| | Square root | Great precision |
| | Narrow | Critical nature |
| | Like letter 'u' | Gentleness |
| | High, rounded starting stroke | Quick, agile mind |
| | Seagull | Easy-going |
| | Extended endstroke | Enterprise |
| | Balanced | A thinker |
| | Elementary | Kindliness |
| | Pointed | Cantankerousness |
| | Simplified | Keen intelligence |
| | Endstroke returning to left | Need for protection |
| | High rounded, endstroke | Pride |
| | Horseshoe | Tendency to prevaricate |
| | Broad, endstroke rising to right | Courage, strength |
| | Very narrow | Shyness |
| | Very broad | Extravagance |
| | Endstroke curling downwards | Calm, serene nature |
| | Rounded | Sincerity |

# W

| | Starting and end-stroke curved in | Tendency to live in the past |
|---|---|---|
| | Crossed in centre | An exhibitionist |
| | Hook on endstroke | Vindictiveness |
| | Small loop on endstroke | Poetic tendencies |
| | Large, with extended endstroke | Ambition |
| | Curved | Love of beauty |
| | Tall starting stroke, low endstroke | Mistrust of others |
| | Long, straight starting line | Aggression |
| | Small circle on starting stroke | Jealousy |
| | Angular | Quick, clear mind |
| | Endstroke curved inwards | Need for protection |
| | Wavy line | Versatility |
| | Full and rounded | Sensitivity |
| | Long starting stroke | Aggression |
| | Two separate strokes | Individualism |
| | Three loops | Vanity |
| | Narrow and angular | Introversion |
| | Balanced and wavy | Artistic talent |
| | Hook on starting stroke | Acquisitiveness |

# X

| | Curved strokes | Team spirit |
|---|---|---|
| | Endstroke underlining word | Self-admiration |
| | Two separate strokes | Pronounced individualism |
| | Claw to left | Egotism, greed |
| | Bow and arrow | Untrustworthiness |
| | Second stroke taller | Enterprise |
| | Second stroke below baseline | Aggression, determination |
| | Loop to left | Quick mind |
| | Knotted in centre | Conscientiousness |
| | Back to back | Mathematical interests |
| | First stroke with pressure | Anger directed towards the past |
| | Split strokes | Perspicacity |
| | Long, straight starting stroke | Resentment, aggression |
| | Curved strokes | Team spirit |
| | Hook on starting and endstroke | Tenacity, obstinacy |
| | Loop to left | Quick mind |
| | Like figure 4 | Calculating attitude |
| | Claw to left | Egotism, greed |
| | Loop on endstroke | Astuteness, cunning |

# Y

| | | |
|---|---|---|
| | Inflated lower loop | Materialism |
| | Arc to left | Fear of responsibility |
| | Like figure 7 | Fatalism |
| | Heavy pressure on downstroke | Cruelty, dissatisfaction |
| | Like capital letter 'X' | Guilt-ridden |
| | Circle on starting stroke | Tendency to create difficulties |
| | Straight downstroke | Agile mind |
| | Hook to left | Avarice |
| | Hook on endstroke | Self-admiration |
| | Two separate strokes | Irrationality |
| | Curled endstroke to left | Team spirit |
| | Like figure 7 (lower case) | Good judgement |
| | Curve to left | Dependence on partner |
| | Wide and looped | Sympathetic, happy nature |
| | Short, pointed endstroke | Sexual repression |
| | Large lower loop | Good sex drive |
| | Unfinished narrow loop | Fear of sex |
| | Unfinished stroke halfway | Difficulty in giving in |
| | Triangle in lower zone | A domestic tyrant |

# Z

| | | |
|---|---|---|
| | Endstroke falling below baseline | Aggression |
| | Very large | Exhibitionism |
| | Tick on starting and endstrokes | Nervousness |
| | Snake-like | Disobedient nature |
| | Top bar removed from stem | High aspirations |
| | Loop on starting stroke | Pride |
| | Curved endstroke | Straightforward nature |
| | Hook on endstroke | Egotism |
| | Top bar to left removed from stem | Disillusionment |
| | Endstroke falling below baseline | Need for protection |
| | Long, straight starting stroke | Romantic nature |
| | Endstroke to left and looped | Unusual erotic interests |
| | Endstroke returning to right | Altruism |
| | Rounded endstroke extended to left | Emotional nature |
| | Unusual shape | Vivid imagination |
| | Like figure 3 | Materialism |
| | Endstroke falling below baseline | Aggression |
| | Looped centre | Determination |
| | Rounded and balanced | Gentle nature |

# Index

Numerals in *italics* refer to illustrations. 'Handwriting' is abbreviated to 'hndw'

## A

'a', the letter 18, 74; as unit of measurement in spacing 54, 55
analysis: exercise for practice in 24–5; rules governing 12, 15; signs, reference list of 65–77
arrogant hndw. 20, 49, *49*, 74
artists *14*, 38, *38*, *61*
aviators *33*

## B

'b', the letter 28
breadth of letters 18
brilliance 38
British Institute of Graphology 9
broad letters 18, *18*, 23, *23*, 66

## C

calmness in rhythm of hndw. 48, *48*, 72
capital letters 13, 22, *22*, 25, 49, 68
Catherine II, *Empress of Russia* 73, *73*
children: concealment 20; disorderly hndw. 40; impatient rhythm 48; meticulous hndw. 41; muddled hndw. 21; obscure hndw. 42; polished hndw. 46; signatures 60; spacing of letters 54; speed of writing 43; systematic inequality 38; wavering hndw. 45
Churchill, Winston 14, *14*
clear hndw. 42, *42*, 72
coherence 35, 42, 56
composers *57*, *67*
concealment, curl of 20, *20*, 68
conformism 28, 30, 41, 59
confusion, curl of 20
connected hndw. 23, 56, 58, 74; *see also* linked hndw., polished hndw.
courtesy 46
Crépieux-Jamin, Jules 7, 29
crossing the 't' 29–31, *29*, *30*, *31*, 50, 68, 71

curls 20, *20*, 48, 50
curving stems 28

## D

'd', the letter 32, *32*, *61*
Dali, Salvador 61, *61*
dictionary of graphology 79–93
dilated hndw. 55, *55*; *see also* disconnected hndw., profuse hndw.
discipline 50
disconnected hndw. 56, 58, 74; *see also* dilated hndw., profuse hndw.
disorderly hndw. 40, *40*, 72; *see also* distorted, muddled, obscure and wavering hndw.
distorted hndw. 16, 20, 66; *see also* disorderly, muddled, obscure and wavering hndw.
dots on 'i's 27, 35, *35*, *70*, 71, 74
downstrokes 32, *32*
dynamic hndw. 44, *44*, 72; *see also* sketchy hndw., speed of writing

## E

envy in love 54
equality (precision in size) 40, 72
even hndw. 59, *59*, 76; *see also* straight hndw.
extensions, upper/lower 32, *32*, 71
extravagance 49

## F

'f', the letter 28, 32
falling hndw. 16, 66; *see also* uneven hndw.
filmstars *31*, *67*, *70*
fleeting gestures 20, *20*, 35
Fleming, Alexander 39, *39*
forced hndw. 16, 66
forenames 60
François I, *King of France* 73, *73*

## G

'g', the letter *24*, 25, 32, *32*, 74

curls 20, *20*, 48, 50

Garbo, Greta 47, *47*
generosity in love 54
graphologists *25*; sign of a good graphologist 23

## H

'h', the letter 28, 32
Hamilton, Lady Emma (portrait) *52*
height of letters 18, *36*
hieroglyphics (Ancient Egypt) *45*
Hitler, Adolf 14, *14*
horizontal strokes 62, 76

## I

'i', the letter 27, 35, *35*, 50, *70*
imagination, lack of 16, 41
impatience in rhythm of hndw. 48, *48*, 72
impulsiveness 29, 40
intelligence 23, 41, 42, 43, 44, 46; dilated hndw. 55; size of letters 38; willpower 12; width of letters 18–9

## J

jealousy in love 54
Jones, Stephen (portrait) *17*

## K

Kant, Immanuel 51, *51*
Karloff, Boris 70, *70*
Kennedy, Jacqueline 13, *13*
Kennedy, John F. 14, *14*

## L

Lady sealing a letter (Chardin) *76*
Leonardo da Vinci 14, *14*
liar, curls of a 29
Lindbergh, Charles 33, *33*
linked hndw. 58, *58*, 76; *see also* connected hndw., polished hndw.
loops, 21, 25, 68
love 35, 44, 46, 53–63; capitals 22; stems and loops, wide-apart 21
loyalty 50
Luttrell psalter *6*

# M

Marat, Jean Paul 13, *13*
Marconi, Guglielmo 19, *19*
marriage 59; signatures of women 60, *60*
Martelli, Diego (portrait of) *75*
Matthew, *Saint* (portrayed) *69*
measurement: letter spacing 54; of percentage of graphological sign 12
meticulous hndw. 35, 41, 72
Michon, Jean Hippolyte 7
monarchs *73*
Mozart, Wolfgang Amadeus 67, *67*
muddled hndw. 21, *21*, 68; *see also* disorderly, distorted, obscure and wavering hndw.
musicians *57, 67*

# N

Napoleon Bonaparte, *Emperor of France* 14, 15, *15*
narrow letters 18, *18*, 68
Nelson, Horatio, letter to Lady Hamilton *63*
Nobel, Alfred 19, *19*

# O

'o', the letter 18, 55
obliteration 62, *62*, 76
obscure hndw. 42, 72; *see also* disorderly, distorted, muddled and wavering hndw.
organization, lack of 40
originality 38, 59

# P

'p', the letter 28, 32, 74
*Palazzo Pretorio* (F. Zandomeneghi) *10*
Pasteur, Louis 39, *39*
pedantry 41, 72
philosophers *51*
plain hndw. 50, 74
polished hndw. 46, *46*, 72; *see also* connected hndw., linked hndw.
Pompeii, painting from *34*
pomposity 49
Powell, William 70, *70*
precise hndw. 20, 43, 46, 50, 74

profuse hndw. 55, *55*, 74; *see also* dilated; disconnected hndw.
psychoanalysis 8
Puccini, Giacomo 57, *57*
Pythagoras (portrayed) *56*

# Q

'q', the letter 13

# R

'r', the letter 74
refinement 41, 46
retraced hndw. 62, 76
rhythm of hndw. 48
Richthofen, *Baron* Manfred von 33, *33*
rising hndw. 16, 66
rules of analysis 12, 15

# S

's', the letter 74
Sanskrit, document written in *64*
scientists *14, 19*, 38, *39*
self-discipline: self-moderation in hndw. 50, *50*, 74
sharp hndw. 18, 28
signatures 14–15, 25; of married women 60, *60*; *see also names of individuals*
signs, graphological: as indication of the good graphologist 23; rules governing 12
size of hndw. 24, 50, 55, 72; *see also* systematic inequality
sketchy hndw. 48, *48*; *see also* dynamic hndw., speed of writing
slanting hndw. 23, 24, *39*, 44, 54, 66, 68, 72; basic rules 16, 28; capitals 22, *22*
slow writing 43, *43*, 72
sobriety, curl of 20
solemn hndw. 49, *49*, 74
spacing: between letters 23, 24–5, 28, 54–5, *54*, *55*, 74; between words 23, 24, 55, *55*, 74
speed of writing 35, 43, *43*, 50, *50*, 72; *see also* dynamic hndw., sketchy hndw.
spiky hndw. 18, *18*
Spinoza, Baruch 51, *51*
stems 16, 21, 23, 25, 28, *28*, 68

straight hndw. 16, 66; *see also* even hndw.
surnames 60, *60*
systematic inequality 23, 37, 38, *38*, 71; *see also* size of hndw.

# T

't', the letter 20, 25, 27, 28, *31*, 50, 68, 71; crossing the 't' 29–31, *29*, *30*, *31*
Taylor, Robert 31, *31*
Temple, Shirley 67, *67*
*Tractatus de Sphera* (de Sacrobosco) *66*
Tracy, Spencer 31, *31*

# U

uneven hndw. 59, *59*, 76; *see also* falling hndw.
upright stems 28, *28*
upstrokes 32, *32*

# V

Valentino, Rudolph 47, *47*
Van Gogh, Vincent 61, *61*
Verdi, Giuseppe 57, *57*
vertical lines 62

# W

wavering hndw. 44–5, 72; *see also* disorderly, distorted, muddled and obscure hndw.
Wells, H. G., (portrait) *36*
wide-apart hndw. 21, *21*, 68
width of letters, compared with height 18
willpower 18, 41, 43, 44, 46, 48, 49; size of letters 38; intellect 12
women 12, 60

# Y

'y', the letter *24*, 25

# Z

'z', the letter 74

# Acknowledgments

Editor: Carolyn Pyrah
Copy Editor: Diana Vowles
Consultant Graphologist: Jane Lyle
Translation: Dawne Roberts/Lesley Bernstein
Art Editor: Brazzle Atkins
Layout: Design 23
Artwork: Brazzle Atkins
Picture Research: Rachel Duffield
Production Controller: Eleanor McCallum

The publishers would like to thank the following for
their kind permission to reproduce the photographs in
this book:

Mary Evans Picture Library 26, 36, 64, 78; Robert Harding
Picture Library 6; Robert Harding Picture Library/British
Museum, London 63; National Portrait Gallery, London 52.